SO-BHX-952

WEIGH the WORD

by CHARLES B. JENNINGS

NANCY KING

and MARJORIE STEVENSON

East Los Angeles Junior College

WEIGH

THE

WORD

HARPER & BROTHERS   PUBLISHERS   NEW YORK

Library of Congress catalog card number: 57–8058

Contents

A LARGER VIEW

Part II. Wherein Are Introduced Standard Makers and Problems of Conformity

WORD MEN

WORD BOOKS

PROBLEMS OF CONFORMITY

Part III. Wherein Are Capriciously Treated Some Profound Problems, and Humor Has Its Say

Preface

Language, the familiar, lightly regarded, seemingly simple tool which makes possible for human beings all communication above the level of gesture, is in reality man's most complex attribute. The sensitive writer, striving to manipulate this tool to create precise meanings, impressions, and moods, is aware of its involved nature and frequent intractability. The linguist, who plots the "family tree" of language relationships, is soon confronted with a maze of branches. The semanticist, who charts and classifies the changes in significations of words, finds himself dealing with problems of almost infinite variations. And certainly most of us, not specialists in the study of words as these others are, occasionally find the use of language in even ordinary situations to be a matter of bewildering intricacy.

The difficult has always intrigued; and the complexities of language have stimulated through centuries the writing of thousands of books, essays, monographs, and articles on almost every conceivable aspect of mankind's means of oral and written communication. The twentieth century, with its ever-widening interest in all facets of human behavior, has produced a rich and widely assorted collection of such studies.

From this assortment the authors have selected samples because of their appeal to the interests of the reader who, though he may not be a specialist in linguistics, is curious about words and language. Though the range of selection is wide, the material has been arranged into three general classifications. Part I contains articles which deal with the problems of the origin and expansion of language, with particular emphasis paid to the current use and misuse of the English tongue and to the wider problem of language as a force for world unity. Part II includes selections concerned with controlling and standardizing language. In them are presented "word men," the compilers of dictionaries, their works, and the problems of conformity to conventional usage. Part III demonstrates that language, though it is a solemn matter to philologists, has its lighter side. In it serious problems are treated with levity which frequently becomes hilarity, ridicule, or satire. Unifying the three parts is the purpose of the selections themselves: to interest, divert, and satisfy the reader who shares with most other people a curiosity about language.

CHARLES B. JENNINGS

February, 1957   NANCY KING

MARJORIE STEVENSON

part I

Wherein Are Presented Beginnings,
Eccentricities, and Future Possibilities

Many Questions and Some Answers

Anyone who is interested in language at all—and who does not possess enough intellectual curiosity to wonder about one of our rarest gifts?—finds himself beset by innumerable questions: Where did speech come from in the beginning? How did men first learn to write? How did places and people and animals get their names? Are the main languages in the world related? Where did our own English come from? How does American-English differ from British-English? How do dialects originate? The list stretches out.

In the following section many of our questions are answered. Some of the answers, of course, must be only speculation; others are a matter of historical record and linguistic research.

"Why should man have a vast language, and animals closely related to him have none at all?" asks Morton M. Hunt, associate editor of *Science Illustrated*. How did language first develop? Where did words come from?

In the following article he discusses the numerous speculations of the philologists to account for the origin of language, including such astonishingly unlikely possibilities as the bow-wow, pooh-pooh, ding-dong, and yo-he-ho theories.

3

Morton M. Hunt

On the Origin of Speeches*

. . . Human language is perhaps mankind's greatest single accomplishment. For many millions of years
animals grunted, shrieked, and yelped by way of simple response to some experience or feeling; but man
took his own vocal possibilities and somehow made of
them a wholly new thing in history—a complete
means of communication.

As a matter of fact, language has an even more basic
value than that of communication: it is an essential to
real thinking, without which there is little to be com-
municated. . . . Man can discuss the past, and plan
for the future; he can talk of hypothetical and unreal
situations, the better to understand the genuine world.
The fourth dimensional space-time continuum, the
Bill of Rights, even a deed to a piece of property—
how could these things have reality except for language? In short, all the major achievements of humanity, and especially the accumulation and passing
down of knowledge, rely on language.

But how did this astonishing and miraculous thing
develop? Who started it? Where did the words come
from? How did things get their names? Who thought
up the need for verbs? How about prepositions? . . .
Why are there so many totally different languages in
the world, anyhow? . . .

. . . The facts themselves can never be obtained.
Unlike the history of dwellings or hand tools or cloth-
ing, the history of language is not marked out by

* Reprinted from "On the Origin of Speeches" by Morton M.
Hunt in *Science Illustrated*, July, 1948, by permission of McGraw-
Hill Publishing Company, Inc.

fossils and preserved objects. Nothing exists in the world to capture for us the sounds, the words, and the first verbal inventions of man's early language. Writing came into the scene only a few thousand years ago—although man has probably been speaking a full language for many thousands of years—so the written word isn't any help in the mystery of how language got started.

One of the most perplexing aspects of the whole problem is the fact that language is exclusively human. Why should man have a vast language, and animals closely related to him have none at all? The anthropologist, Earnest Hooton, has pointed out that although speech is a function of man's developed brain, there is no specific feature or part of man the absence of which accounts for the lack of language in the apes. "Even the so-called speech area, the third inferior frontal convolution of Broca," he says, "is distinguishable in the brains of chimpanzees and gorillas."

Some people have argued that animals *do* have language, and that man's speech developed simply by a slow process of mimicry and evolution. Man supposedly imitated the characteristic sound of a certain animal, in order to tell his neighbor something about that animal. A bark or roar would signify a dog or a lion, and the different kinds of animal sounds—whining, yelping, angry barking—were imitated by primitive man to give different shades of meaning.

Max Mueller, a waggish German philologist of the last century, irreverently dubbed this the "bow-wow" theory, and it has never been the same since. There are good reasons why it is totally inadequate. It can explain only a tiny percentage of words in human speech, and it certainly gives all the credit of creating language to the animals. Man did nothing but imitate the animal language—a psychologically improbable premise. Even more damaging is the simple fact that words which signify a given animal are completely unlike in various languages throughout the world; yet the animals themselves make exactly the same sounds. A cat anywhere says approximately, "maiow." But there are hundreds of entirely dissimilar words for "cat" in the world's more than two thousand languages. . . .

Another school of thought in the last century held that language began with instinctive utterances called forth by pain, surprise, fear, or other intense sensations and emotions. These sounds are mainly interjections of modern speech, such as *ouch, oh, ah, whee, tsk,* and *yi.* Charles Darwin tried to explain how these sounds came to exist. He said that when there is a feeling of contempt or disgust, it is accompanied by a tendency to "blow out of the mouth or nostrils, and this produces sounds like *pooh* or *pish.*" Naturally enough, the dignified and scientific label "interjectional theory" soon was replaced by the nickname, "pooh-pooh" theory.

The pooh-pooh theory was dismissed by later philologists as being a piffling idea. Like the bow-wow, it explained only a very small handful of words in the human languages. Even more to the point, the interjectional words thus created are quite isolated from the vast bulk of language. They fail to take part in real grammatical sentences, and usually stand alone as expressions of some simple emotion. In fact, says the great Scandinavian scholar, Jespersen, there is such a chasm between the pooh-pooh words and other words that they can often be considered as the negation of real language—for they are used when one cannot or will not use real language. . . .

A far more comprehensive theory was trotted out by the nature-lovers of the nineteenth century. There is a mystic harmony, they said, between sound and sense; when primitive man saw or experienced anything, a simple reflex action caused certain sounds to arise to his lips. Max Mueller, originator of this "naturistic" theory, claimed that there was a law in nature that everything which is struck rings with its own individual sound. Language is the peculiar and individual ring or sound each thing has—when observed by man. The nickname for Mueller's theory was obvious from the start—it became known as the "ding-dong" theory.

Actually, Mueller's concept was one of the oldest. The unknown author of Genesis had recorded the ancient Hebrew theory of language in Chapter 2, Verses 19 and 20. "And out of the ground the Lord God formed every beast of the field, and every fowl of the air; and brought them unto Adam to see what he would call them: and whatsoever Adam called every living creature, that was the name thereof." The scene, to interpolate a bit, must have been about like this: The animals were led past Adam, who had never seen them before nor known any words for them. As the first came past, Adam said, "I'll call that a *bear*, and the next one is a *lion*, and the next one a *cow*." If the Lord or any angel had asked him why the first was a bear and the second a lion, instead of the other way around, he would undoubtedly have answered, "Why, because the first one *looks like* bear—it has *bearness*; and the second one *looks like* lion. It's really very simple."

Today, nobody pays any attention to the ding-dong. Modern psychology has observed that only a few kinds of baby sounds are made by the infant, and they never show any pattern. Tables don't call forth the sound *table* from the child's mouth. Even more obvious, there are many unrelated languages of the world, with vocabularies entirely unlike each other's. Does this mean that the primitive responses to an experience were different in different lands? Why should a European Neanderthal man look at a tree, and suddenly utter a different sound from that of another Neanderthal man living in Asia?

Even more foolish than the bow-wow, pooh-pooh, or ding-dong, was the theory of language origins started by the German philosopher Ludwig Noire, and dignified with the impressive title of *Die Arbeitstheorie*—the work theory. Language began, Noire thought, with the natural sounds that man produced while working or performing any muscular effort. Under such muscular effort, it is a relief to let the breath come out strongly and repeatedly, thus vibrating the vocal chords and making sounds. The first words spoken would therefore be such expressions as *heave*, *haul*, or *push*. Naturally enough *Arbeitstheorie* was soon unofficially known as the "yo-he-ho" theory.

The yo-he-ho, quite clearly, explains even fewer words than any of the other partial theories. It is slightly more believable than the ding-dong, but far less satisfying, for it hardly advances language history beyond the animal level. Its chief use in recent years has been to add a note of humor to otherwise stuffy philology lectures.

All such speculation was abruptly junked about a generation ago when the scholarly Otto Jespersen announced a completely new point of view in language study. He said that philologists had been indulging in armchair philosophizing for too long, and trying to deduce the origins of language by pure reason. Jespersen himself felt that a far more scientific method would be to take modern languages as they are, compare them with those same languages as they were in previous centuries, and thus learn what kind of changes took place. Having learned these laws of change, he could then estimate what primitive languages were like. And enough primitive languages still exist today to help check the results.

The method was extremely fruitful in some respects, but for those who wanted a real answer as to how speech got started, the mystery became even more confusing. For older forms of the languages known today were far more difficult than their modern descendants; and the languages of primitive and barbaric peoples are frequently harder to learn and more complex than Latin, Greek, or Sanskrit. If this is true, then man appears not to have begun with a simple speech, and gradually made it more complex, but rather to have gotten hold of a tremendously knotty speech somewhere in the unrecorded past, and gradually simplified it to the modern forms. This is strangely contrary to the usual kind of development in human culture, and it is no wonder that the Jespersen theories—though excellent for philologists in general—were little comfort to fireside philosophers. . . .

Today's books on language and human speech de-
vote only a few cautious pages to the whole problem,
and philologists prefer to dodge the matter altogether
whenever they can. The way in which men got their
speech, and where this happened—and when—will
probably remain among the mysteries of science that
will never be solved.

In remote prehistoric days when men first moved out
across a land without names, how did they come to settle upon just this name for this mountain and just that
name for that stream? In this excerpt from his book
Names on the Land, George Stewart (professor of
English at the University of California and author of
Storm, Fire, Man, US 40, and *American Ways of Life*)
reconstructs imaginatively how the first naming may
have come about.

GEORGE R. STEWART

Of the Naming That Was Before History*

In the distant past, then, the land was without
names. Yet the nature of the land itself prefigured
something of what was to be. Where jagged mountains reared up along the horizon, many names would
describe shapes, but in a flat country names of other
meanings would be given. Where most streams were
clear but one ran thick with reddish mud, a man coming to that stream would call it Red River, whether he
said Rio Colorado, or Rivière Rouge, or Bogue Homa,
or blurted syllables in some now long-forgotten tongue.

* Reprinted from *Names on the Land* by George R. Stewart, by
permission of Houghton Mifflin Company. Copyright 1954 by
Houghton Mifflin Company.

Since alders first grew close to water and desert-cedars clung to hillsides, they predestined Alder Creek and Cedar Mountain. Long Lake and Stony Brook, Blue Ridge and Grass Valley, lay deeper than tribe or language; the thing and the name were almost one.

No one knows when man came, or who gave the first names. Perhaps the streams still ran high from the melting ice-cap, and strange beasts roamed the forest. And since names—corrupted, transferred, re-made—outlive men and nations and languages, it may even be that we still speak daily some name which first meant "Saber-tooth Cave" or "Where-we-killed-the-ground-sloth."

There is no sure beginning. At the opening of history many and various tribes already held the land, and had given it a thin scattering of names. The names themselves can be made to reveal the manner of the earliest naming.

Once, let us say, some tribesmen moved toward a new country, which was unknown to them. Halting, they chose a good man, and sent him ahead. This scout went on, watching not to be ambushed or get lost, knowing he must report shrewdly when he returned. First he skulked along the edge of a big meadow, where he saw many deer. Then he came to a stream where he noted some oak trees, which were uncommon in that country. All this time he was skirting the slope of a great mountain, but because he was actually on it, and because the trees were so thick, he did not think of a mountain; and, besides, it made no difference to him one way or the other. So he went farther on—through a little swamp, and to a stream which he crossed on a beaver-dam. This stream was the same as the one where the oak trees grew, but he had no way of being certain, and besides it did not matter at all—each crossing was a thing in itself. He went on, through a narrow defile with many tall rocks, which he knew would be an ugly spot for an ambush. Going back, he noted all the places in reverse, but did not actually bestow any names on them.

When he told his story, however, he unconsciously gave names by describing places, such as the big meadow and the stream where the oak trees grew. He did not speak of the mountain, because the mountain was everywhere and the whole country was merely its slope; and he did not speak of the deer in the meadow, because he knew that deer are at one place for sun-up and another for nooning, so that only a fool would try to distinguish one meadow from another by mentioning them.

The others listened to his words, nodded and questioned and remembered; they knew that they would have no other knowledge of the next day's march, and that life and death might hang on how well they remembered his landmarks. So they thought to themselves, "big meadow," "stream where oak trees grow," "stream with a beaver-dam," and the rest. When they went ahead into that country, they recognized each place as they came to it.

Then, when they lived there, they used the descriptions first, saying, "There is good fishing in the stream where oak trees grow." But soon they said, "stream-where-oak-trees-grow" in one breath, and it had become a name.

The first simple names were like sign-posts, noting something permanent and easily recognized, something to distinguish one place from other places—size, or shape, or color, or the kind of rocks or trees found there. After the tribe grew familiar with the region, such sign-post names were no longer much needed, and as the people began to have memories of what had happened here or there, names of another kind sprang up.

At some stream, perhaps, a hunter saw a panther drinking in broad daylight, and killed it with a single arrow. This was a matter of wonder, and people began to say: "the stream where the panther was killed." After a few generations the actual story may have been forgotten, but the name retained. In the old Choctaw country there is still a Quilby Creek, from their words *koi-ai-albi*, "panther-there-killed." Far in the Southwest a ruined pueblo is Callemongue, "where-they-hurled-down-stones." But the name is the only testimony; no man knows the story of that desperate siege, or who hurled down stones at what besiegers.

Not all these adventures need have been real. If a young man saw a vision, what happened to him then may have been as vivid as the killing of a panther. Or he may have thought that his dream made manifest the world of spirits. So in the country of the Sioux many places had the suffix *-wakan*, and among the Algonquians *-manito*, to show that a presence haunted them. . . .

If a tribe lived in the same region for many generations, the name-pattern grew more complex. The land itself might change. Stream-with-a-Beaver-Dam might fill with silt and become a mere swamp, so that the beavers no longer lived there. The dam itself would be grown over with trees and bushes. After the dam became indistinguishable, the name was actually misleading. Then it might be changed entirely, but a traditional-minded tribe would sometimes keep the old name, as in a modern city Canal Street may remain after the canal has long been filled in.

Language also changed with the generations, and names more rapidly than the rest of language. A lengthy descriptive name of an important place was said so often that it was likely to be clipped and slurred. Before long, it sounded like words having some other meaning, or else like meaningless syllables. The tribe had no written records to show what the name should be. Eventually some story-teller might build up a tale to explain the new name. Thus Allegheny seems most likely to have meant "fine river" in the language of the Delawares, but they later told a story of a myth-ical tribe called the Allegewi who had lived on that river until defeated by the all-conquering Delawares. More often, when a common name became meaning-less, the Indians, like other people, merely accepted it —"Just a name!"

"Ja, Mutter, ich habe drei," says the German child. "Si, madre (yo) tengo tres," says the Spanish child. "Yes, Mother, I have three," says the English child. It is clear, even to those of us who do not know German or Spanish well, that some relationship must exist to ac-count for the similarities among these three languages.

In the following article Margaret Schlauch (professor of English, New York University, and author of Saga of the Volsungs and Romance in Iceland) explains the methods used in the study of comparative linguistics to prove that German, Spanish, English, and many other languages have developed through the centuries from a single ancient language—the parent Indo-European.

Margaret Schlauch

Family Relationships Among Languages*

Let us take a single sentence and follow its land-changes, its mutations, over a fairly wide territory—as territories are reckoned in Europe.

Suppose you begin a trip in Sweden, and you find yourself seated with a mother who is anxiously supervising the box lunch of several small children. She turns solicitously to one of them and says, "Did you get any cookies (or apples, or candies)?" And the child replies: "Yes, Mother, I have three." In Swedish that would be, "*Ja, moder, jag har tre.*" In Norway, to the west, or Denmark, to the south, it would be almost the same: "*Jà, mor, jeg har tre.*"

The slight differences in vowel sound and in sentence melody do not disguise the fact that we are listening to the same words. A moment's reflection will suggest the right explanation. We are not confronted by a borrowing or "mixture" in any case. The three Scandinavian languages mentioned are equally ancient. At one time they were identical, for all practical purposes. A traveler in olden times (let us say the ninth century) could traverse the whole length of Norway or Sweden and pass to the southern extremity of Denmark without any change in his speech. Everywhere he would hear children say: "*Já, móðir, ek hefi þrjá.*" (The last word was pronounced [θrja:].) The changes and differences developed during centuries, rather rapidly in Denmark, more slowly in Sweden.

* *The Gift of Tongues* by Margaret Schlauch. Copyright 1942 by Margaret Schlauch. Reprinted by permission of The Viking Press, Inc., New York.

As a result, we now have diversity where once there was unity. Three national languages, equally venerable, have replaced Old Scandinavian. They are extremely close relatives, but none could claim parental precedence over the others. If any branch of Scandinavian could exact respect on the grounds of conservatism (that is, fidelity to the parent, the Old Scandinavian) it would be modern Icelandic, spoken in the distant island which Norwegians settled in the ninth century. Here children still say: *"Já, móđir, ek hefi þrjá."* The values of the vowels have changed slightly; that is all.

When the train crosses from Denmark into Germany, a greater change becomes apparent. Here the maternal inquiry elicits the answer, *"Ja, Mutter, ich habe drei."* In Holland or the Flemish-speaking parts of Belgium, tow-headed lads murmur, *"Ja, moeder* (or *moer) ik heb er drie."* The cleavage is greater, but the separate words still look distinctly familiar. We can even group the versions of our little sentence to show where two or more languages show particular likeness:

Icelandic:	*Já, móđir, ek hefi þrjá.*
Swedish:	*Ja, moder, jag har tre.*
Danish:	*Ja, mor, jeg har tre.*
Norwegian:	*Ja, mor, jeg har tre.*
German:	*Ja, Mutter, ich habe drei.*
Dutch:	*Ja, moeder, ik heb drie.*
Flemish:	*Ja, moeder, ik heb drie.*
English:	Yes, mother, I have three.

German stands somewhat apart because its consonants show certain peculiarities: it alone has a [t] between vowels (that is, intervocalic) in the word for mother.

Still, it is clear that we are still dealing with variations on the same theme.

Just as the Scandinavian examples revealed close kinship among themselves, so all of those in the extended list show some degree of relationship with one another. Sentences betraying the close linguistic ties within this same group could be multiplied indefinitely. Such being the case, we are justified in speaking of a "family" of languages, borrowing a metaphor from the realm of human relations.

Parent Germanic

Detailed comparisons of this sort indicate that all the members of this Germanic group go back to a single parent language, now lost, spoken as a unity somewhere between the first century B.C. and the first A.D. We call this lost parent language Primitive Germanic. Its modern descendants are grouped into what is known as the Germanic families of European languages. English is one of them. The precise geographical location of Primitive Germanic is not known. We can surmise the nature of its sounds (*phonology*) and inflections (*morphology*) with what is probably fair accuracy, however, because of some early literature and inscriptions dating back to a time when the separate descendants had as yet separated very little from one another. The runic inscription on the Gallebus horn . . . belongs to this early period. It was Old Scandinavian, but it might almost have been composed in an early form of any of the others mentioned.

By comparative study it has been established which sounds in the quoted words are most faithful to the original language. We know that English has preserved the initial consonant of the word "three" [θ] as spoken in Primitive Germanic; but that Icelandic, Flemish, and Dutch have kept the consonant at the end of the first person pronoun singular (*ik*), which has been lost in English and transformed in the others. Back of the multiplicity of extant forms we can feel our way to the existence of the single speech called parent Germanic.

Romance Languages

But now let us continue the journey south. In Belgium our anxious Flemish mother may be replaced by a fellow-countrywoman who speaks French. Her child will say something strikingly different from anything heard so far: "*Oui, mère* (or *maman*), *j'en ai trois.*" As the train goes southwards towards that fertile cradle of cultures, the Mediterranean basin, it may be routed towards the Pyrenees, or across the Alps into Italy. If it should cross the Iberian peninsula you would hear in Spain: "*Sí, madre,* (*yo*) *tengo tres*; and in Portugal: "*Sim, mãe, tenho tres.*" But if it should take you across the barrier which Hannibal—even Hannibal—found all but impassable, down the steep slopes to the smiling Lombard plains, you would hear: "*Si, madre, ce n'ho tre.*" And even across the Adriatic, on the far side of the Balkan peninsula, hardy descendants of the Roman army and Roman colonists will be saying in Rumanian: "*Da, mama mea, eu am trei.*"

The similarities are apparent:

French:	*Oui, mère, j'en ai trois.*
Spanish:	*Sí, madre,* (*yo*) *tengo tres.*
Portuguese:	*Sim, mãe, tenho tres.*
Italian:	*Si, madre, ce n'ho tre.*
Rumanian:	*Da, mama mea, eu am trei.*

The situation is comparable to the one which diverted and possibly mystified you in Germanic territory. You have been traversing lands where the people communicate with one another in tongues clearly descended from a single parent. This time the parent language was a form of Latin: not the solemn speech, stilted and formal, which was reserved for polite literature and speeches in the forum, but the popular or "vulgar" Latin spoken by common people throughout the length and breadth of the Roman territory. Plain soldiers, tavern keepers, itinerant merchants, freedmen, small traders, naturalized citizens of all the polyglot Roman provinces, must have used this form of discourse as an international *lingua franca*. In this idiom they bought and sold, exchanged jokes, flirted, lamented, and consoled with one another. We know from late written documents and inscriptions (especially those on the humbler tombstones of poor folk) just how ungrammatical, rapid, informal, and even slangy this Latin was, compared with the intricate and highly mannered periods of a Cicero. People had become impatient with the many case endings required in classical Latin, and were reducing them to two or three. Even these were treated with a playful carelessness. The verb was handled in a different way—a more vivid one—to show changes in tense; and the word order was simplified. Moreover, slang words triumphed completely over traditional ones in some provinces. Ordinary people in Gaul (perhaps emulating the jargon of the army) stopped referring to the human head as *caput*, and substituted *testa* or "pot," from which comes modern French *tête*. It is as if all persons speaking English should have fallen into the way of saying "my bean" for the same object, so that it became the accepted word, while "head" was lost entirely.

The popular Roman speech differed from one province to another because popular locutions do tend always to be regional, and because the Romans came in contact with widely differing types of native speech. Thus the pronunciation and even the grammar were affected by the underlying populations. In one place the Latin word *habēre* continued to be used for "to have"; in the Spanish peninsula, however, it so happened that *tenēre*, meaning "to hold," came to be used in its place in the more general sense of "to have." That is why our imaginary Spanish child says *tengo* instead of any form of the classical *habēre*. The number "three," on the other hand, varies only slightly in the series of Romance sentences quoted. The numbers have remained fairly stable in the various daughter languages perpetuated from Vulgar Latin. One of the factors tending to preserve a similarity in them throughout the ages has been their similar experience in developing a strong stress accent during the transition to the Middle Ages. This new accentuation caused similar losses in unaccented syllables in a given word in all Mediterranean areas. There were differences, of course, in the forms that emerged; but certainly not enough to make the results unrecognizably alien to one another.

The neo-Latin languages (if the expression may be permitted) give us another example, therefore, of a family which bears its signs of consanguinity very legibly on the external aspect of each of its members. In Roman times, Latin itself could claim cousins (in the ancient *Italic* group) which have since been lost.

The Slavic Family

And here is one further example of language relationship which may metaphorically be called close consanguinity. In eastern Europe a sharp-eared traveler on an international train will also have an opportunity to detect fundamental similarity behind the changing visages of national speech. A far-flung territory is occupied by peoples speaking *Slavic* languages and dialects. It would be possible to pursue the transformation of our key sentence addressed to an imaginary Slavic mother to the east as follows:

Czechish: *Ano, matko, mam tři.*
Polish: *Tak, matko, mam trzy.*
Russian: *Da, mat', u men'á tri.*

When our international train crosses into the Soviet Union, it will pass through various sections of Russia showing distinct dialect colorings. Ukrainian, for instance, shows enough differentiation to be dignified as a national language, with an official spelling of its own. Even an untutored eye, however, can see how close it is to the official language of Great Russia, the classical medium of literature known to the world as "Russian." In the Balkan states, South Slavic languages show these perceptible nuances of our chosen theme. For instance, the Bulgarian version of it would be: "*Da, maika, imom tri.*"

Once again, we are justified in assuming that centuries ago there was a single language from which these cousins descended. About the seventh century it was probably still fairly unified. In the ninth century a southern dialect of this early Slavic (Old Bulgarian)

was written down in a translation of the Bible made
by Saints Cyril and Methodius. The text helps us to
get quite a clear picture of parent Slavic, just as runic
inscriptions bring us close to Primitive Germanic, and
unofficial documents of the Roman Empire tell us
much about Vulgar Latin.

Indo-European, Parent of Parents

Slavic, Romance, and Germanic represent three
families of languages spoken in Europe today. But
surely it must be clear that similarities link these families to one another besides linking the smaller sub-
divisions within each given family. In *all* the national
languages surveyed so far, it will be noticed, the word
for "mother" began with the labial nasal [m]; in a
considerable number a dental [t], [đ], or [d] appeared in the middle of the word after the first vowel.
Likewise in *all* of the languages listed, "three" began
with a dental [t], [d], or [θ], followed by an [r].
Why is this?

Clearly, at a still earlier period than the days of
early (prehistoric) Germanic and Slavonic, and of
Vulgar Latin, there must have been a more ancient
and inclusive unity which embraced all three.

The same procedure, if pursued farther, would have
revealed to us other major families belonging to the
same larger embracing unity in Europe and parts of
Asia. These are:

Celtic, including Irish, Highland Scottish, Welsh,
and Breton. (In modern Irish, "mother" is *mathair*
and "three" is *tri*.)

Baltic, including Lettish, Lithuanian, and an extinct
dialect once spoken in the territory of modern Prussia
(Old Prussian). The word for "mother" is *motina*,

not closely related to the cognates already cited. *Tris* for "three" is, on the other hand, an obvious cognate.

Hellenic, including modern Greek dialects, some of which go back to very ancient times. (An ancient Greek dialect, Attic, spoken in the city of Athens, produced a body of literature of enduring splendor. Its word for "mother" was *matér* and for "three," *treîs.* This is the classical language studied in school.)

Albanian, the national language of Albania, with no close relatives outside its own borders. Here "three" is *tre;* but the word for "mother" is not related to the forms in the above languages. A new form, *nona,* has replaced the Indo-European term preserved elsewhere.

Armenian, spoken in Armenia (between Europe and Asia Minor), is, like Albanian, a language with many diverse elements borrowed from outside, but it has an independent history traceable back to the fifth or sixth century A.D. Its word for "mother," *mair,* is easily recognizable as a cognate of the others given; not so, however, is *erek* for "three."

Even in Asia there are languages with venerable histories and rich literary heritage which can be recognized as members of the same linguistic clan:

Indian, including Hindustani, Bengali, Marathi, and Hindi. These dialects are descended from Old Indian, preserved to us in a classical literary form (Sanskrit) which dates back to the fifteenth century B.C. or even several hundred years earlier. Sanskrit, despite its great antiquity, still shows close generic resemblance to its modern European cousins. Its word for "mother" was *mātṛ* and for "three," *tri.*

Iranian, very closely related to Sanskrit, was spoken in the Persian highlands while Indian was spreading

over the interior of India. It produced an early literature in the form of Zoroastrian hymns. Since those
ancient times Persian has been subjected to large foreign infiltration, notably Arabic, but its structure still
reveals its kinship with the other groups listed.

Hittite, a language spoken by people frequently mentioned in the Bible, is now extinct. Cuneiform inscriptions give us enough material to reveal its fundamental
character. Some sort of relationship it surely must have
had with the members of the broad family of families
now being surveyed, but the precise nature of that relationship is still under discussion.

Tocharian, now extinct, is represented by some frag-
mentary texts (probably antedating the tenth century),
which were discovered in eastern Turkestan in a Bud-
dhist monastery. The material is too scanty to permit
of definitive analysis, but it shows relationship to the
above subsidiary groups.

Our railroad trip beginning with Germanic territory
has taken us far afield, even to the shores of the Indus
River in Asia. Even so, and despite the most baffling
diversities, skilled comparison of key words has been
able to establish that the miniature families surveyed
do undoubtedly belong to the same large, inclusive
family already postulated to account for likenesses observed among Germanic, Slavonic, and Romance
(from Old Italic).

Back of the smaller families lay a single family; attached to this single family it is almost certain there
must have been a single language. We call the whole
family by the name "Indo-European," a term generally preferred today to "Indo-Germanic" or "Aryan,"
both of which could easily be misunderstood. That is

to say, every language mentioned so far is an Indo-European language, no matter what smaller group it may belong to.

Homeland of Indo-European

But if they are all related thus, we must assume that a single definite language, parent Indo-European, gave rise to all of them. This is probably true. Some time before 2000 B.C., in some part of the world, a group which was essentially a single community spoke this single parent language. Later, dialect forms of this tribal language were carried into many different countries, from Iceland to India—by emigration, by conquest, by peaceful transfer. We do not know how this occurred in every case, but the expansion had already begun in earliest historical times.

Where the parent language was spoken, and by whom, is something of a mystery. By studying words that are common to a number of the family groups listed above we can, to be sure, get some idea of the culture these people had before their language was spread over a wide area and differentiated by the divisions, migrations, or conquests of a half-dozen millennia ago. We can surmise that they probably lived in a temperate climate because a number of the descended languages have similar words for spring, summer, autumn, and winter. There are common words indicating a developed (though still simple) agriculture: terms having to do with the plow, spade, sickle, and mill; with carting, sowing, and mowing. For instance, the word for plow is *arðr* in Icelandic, *áratron* in Greek, *arātrum* in Latin, *arathar* in Irish, *árklas* in Lithuanian, *araur* in Armenian. The names of certain plants and animals are supposed to offer some guidance. Parent Indo-European had terms for dogs, cows, sheep, bulls, goats, pigs, and horses; also for wild animals such as the bear, the wolf, and the fox. Hermann Hirt, author of an elaborate discussion of the subject, considers the common words for "eel" in several languages as very important. If the original speakers of Indo-European knew this fish, they could not have lived originally near the Black Sea, where it is not found. Another important word is the old term for the beech tree in the various languages. The words *Buche* in German, *fagus* in Latin, *Bachenis* Forest in a Celtic place-name, and *Phegós* (φηγός) in Greek (where it had been transferred, however, to the oak tree), indicate that the beech was a tree known at the time of the parent language. The forms just quoted could all have come from a single root. Now the eastern boundary for the presence of this European tree is a line drawn roughly from Königsberg to the Crimea. Therefore Hirt argues that the parent language must have developed to the west of such a line.

North central Germany, Lithuania, the Danube Valley, and Southern Russia (near the Black Sea) have been suggested in turn as the original homeland of the parent language. India, once regarded as the cradle of our general Indo-European speech, has been relinquished in favor of European territories answering to the geographical clues of the joint vocabularies. Of these it may be said that probability favors those districts in which there are many physical traces of early mankind, such as burial mounds, skeletons, fragments of pottery, signs of human habitation. The Danube Valley is particularly rich in these, and also Germany and Southern Russia. Lithuania can boast an extraordinarily archaic language, similar in many ways to ancient Sanskrit, but its territory is poor in archaeological remains, those mute witnesses to the daily living of people like ourselves who "flourished" (if that is the proper word) in prehistoric times. Lithuania may have been settled early in the age that saw the spread of Indo-European, but it is less likely than other districts to have seen its first development.

No matter where Indo-European developed out of still earlier linguistic stages now hopelessly lost, it is important to remember that we know absolutely nothing about the physical appearance of its first speakers. They have long since been leveled with the dust; we cannot say whether their skin was light or dark, their vanished hair shadowy or bright. Among the broad-skulled and long-skulled and medium-skulled remains of prehistoric men, we cannot tell which—if any—moved their bony jaws in olden times to the sounds and rhythms of the Indo-European parent language. Although most of the contemporary peoples of Europe may be descendants, in part, of members of our postulated Indo-European community, still it is not safe to assume that this community was itself racially homogeneous. . . .

At the moment, however, what interests us most is the evidence of underlying unity, not of divergence in the Indo-European family. As we shall see, the divergences turn out to be fairly regular when they are closely examined. Because they are more or less predictable by an advanced student, they do not disturb seriously his impressions of the underlying unity which justifies him in regarding the whole majestic array of tongues as a close-knit family. The more acutely one observes the principles of correspondence and divergence, the easier it becomes to learn a new member within the widely scattered group.

Cursory as this review has been, it has probably indicated the approach and even something of the methods used in the study of comparative linguistics. . . .

Using the methods just described by Margaret Schlauch, comparative linguistics has been able to establish, too, family groupings for most of the languages of the world. In the following chart Frederick Bodmer, philologist, lists for us the principal language groups.

(Bodmer and Lancelot Hogben, editor of *The Loom of Language*, first conceived the idea of their book while they were colleagues at the University of Capetown.)

FREDERICK BODMER

The Loom of Language*

The Indo-European or Aryan group does not include all existing European languages. . . .

Something like a hundred language groups, including the Papuan, Australian and Amerindian (e.g. Mexican and Greenlandic) vernaculars, Japanese, Basque, Manchu, Georgian, and Korean, still remain to be connected in larger units. This has not been possible so far, either because they have not yet been properly studied, or because their past phases are not on record. Below is a list of families which are well-defined:

* Reprinted from *The Loom of Language* by Frederick Bodmer by permission of W. W. Norton & Company, Inc. Copyright 1944 by W. W. Norton & Company, Inc.

I. INDO-EUROPEAN:

(a) *Teutonic*
> (German, Dutch, Scandinavian, English)

(b) *Celtic*
> (Erse, Gaelic, Welsh, Breton)

(c) *Romance*
> (French, Spanish, Catalan, Portuguese, Italian, Rumanian)

(d) *Slavonic*
> (Russian, Polish, Czech, Slovakian, Bulgarian, Serbo-Croatian, and Slovene)

(e) *Baltic*
> (Lithuanian, Lettish)

(f) *Greek*

(g) *Albanian*

(h) *Armenian*

(i) *Persian*

(j) *Modern Indic dialects*

II. FINNO-UGRIAN:

(a) *Lappish*

(b) *Finnish*

(c) *Esthonian*

(d) *Cheremissian, Mordvinian*

(e) *Magyar (Hungarian)*

III. SEMITIC:

(a) *Arabic*

(b) *Ethiopian*

(c) *Hebrew*

(d) *Maltese*

IV. HAMITIC:

      (a) *Cushite (Somali, Galla)*
      (b) *Berber* languages

V. INDO-CHINESE:

      (a) *Chinese*
      (b) *Tibetan*
      (c) *Siamese*
      (d) *Burmese*

VI. MALAYO-POLYNESIAN:

      (a) *Malay*
      (b) *Fijian*
      (c) *Tahitian*
      (d) *Maori*

VII. TURCO-TARTAR:

      (a) *Turkish*
      (b) *Tartar*
      (c) *Kirghiz*

VIII. DRAVIDIAN:

      (a) *Tamil*
      (b) *Telugu*
      (c) *Canarese*

IX. BANTU:

      Kafir, Zulu, Bechuana, Sesuto, Herero, Congo, Duala, etc.

In some instances a few tongues, shown with their relatives in the principal language groups charted by Bodmer in the preceding selection, tend to be coalesced by borrowing into the making of an almost completely new language. To a degree this fact can be seen in Eng-

lish, as Stuart Robertson and Frederic G. Cassidy demonstrate in tracing its development from the early to
the modern period.

STUART ROBERTSON, REVISED BY
FREDERIC G. CASSIDY

The Early Growth of English*

Languages are studied historically according to the
"periods" of their development, during which they
exhibit distinguishing characteristics; thus, English is
divided into the Old, Middle, and Modern periods.
Obviously, such a division, while convenient, is arbitrary, since people do not leave off speaking one form
of a language one night and start speaking another
form the next day. Though it does not go always at
the same pace, language development is continuous.
The division into periods is made when the historical
linguist, looking backward, sees that by about a certain date the gradual changes have mounted up until
the language as a whole is decidedly different, or has
entered a new phase of development. We shall date the
periods of English as follows:

Old English	450–1100
Middle English	1100–1500
Modern English	1500–the present

The history of the English language begins, then,
with the incursions of the Jutes, Saxons, and Angles
about the middle of the fifth century. These invaders
came from neighboring regions in what is now Schles-

* Reprinted by permission of the publisher from *The Develop-
ment of Modern English*, 2nd ed., by Stuart Robertson, revised by
Frederic G. Cassidy. Copyright 1934, 1938, 1954, by Prentice-Hall,
Inc., Englewood Cliffs, N.J.

wig-Holstein; they spoke, not one language, but related Low German dialects. The Jutes came first and occupied the smallest territory, principally Kent and the Isle of Wight. The Saxons occupied practically all of England south of the Thames, with the exception of these Jutish territories, and of Cornwall, which remained in the possession of the Celts; north of the Thames they also occupied the regions which later became Essex and Middlesex (the final syllables of which still bear the Saxon name). The Angles took for themselves what was left: the greatest part of what is now England, and Lowland Scotland as far as the Firth of Forth, with the exception of the west coast.

Here then is the explanation of the division of Old English into dialects that have left their trace in the provincial speech of England until this day. The dialectal groupings have been somewhat shifted, but a threefold division is still preserved. The speech of the Jutes became the Kentish dialect of Old English; the principal dialect of the Saxons was known as the West Saxon; and the Anglian tongue split into two dialects, the Mercian in the Midlands and the Northumbrian in the North . . . ; the Northumbrian became the Northern, the popular tongue on both sides of the Scottish border.

Literary supremacy has swung from the North to the South and eventually come to the Midland. In Old English times the first centers of learning and culture were in Northumbria; the first important literature in English, dating from the seventh and early eighth centuries, was therefore in the Northumbrian dialect. By the end of the ninth century another center was established, in the south, in Alfred's kingdom of Wessex—therefore the body of later Old English literature is in this West Saxon dialect. In Middle English times, no one dialect could claim to be supreme until the East Midland (and specifically the dialect of London) finally asserted itself by the end of the fourteenth century as the most favored. Standard Modern English represents, for the most part, the further development of this dialect—which has not been, however, without important rivalry from the Northern, particularly in the late Middle and early Modern periods.

To outline the general development of the language in its Old and Middle periods requires us to return to pre-Saxon Britain, and to retell a familiar story. When the Germanic invaders came, Britain was inhabited by the Celts, who had dwelt there for centuries. Their language, too, was Indo-European, but the Celtic and Germanic branches were by this time so far differentiated as to have little in common. Celtic Britain had been invaded by the Romans in 55 and 54 B.C., as we are told in the *Commentaries* of Julius Caesar, but no serious attempt to conquer the island was made till almost a century later. By the end of the first century A.D., however, the conquest was complete, and a Roman colony which embraced the territory as far north as what is now Lowland Scotland was established. This military occupation of Britain lasted until the early fifth century, when the far-flung Roman legions began to be withdrawn from the provinces to defend the capital against attack by the barbarian Goths. Britain, the most distant western outpost of the empire, was the first to be abandoned. The Celtic inhabitants, left defenseless against the attacks of the Picts and Scots on the west and north, appealed in vain to Rome for help. At last they called in the aid of the Germanic sea-rovers who had in the past harried their shores. The call was answered; but the upshot was disastrous to the Celts, for the Germanic tribes who came to help against the Picts and Scots soon coveted the island for themselves, turned against their Celtic allies, and succeeded in dispossessing them of the greater part of their lands.

. . . The influence of the earlier languages of the island—Celtic and Latin—upon the invaders . . . was slight: the Celtic influence has never been great; the important Latin influences began later. The Celts were either the subjects or the enemies of the Anglo-Saxons, the Celtic border-chieftains often helping the Danes later in their attacks on the English. Nor should it be forgotten that the word "Welsh" is not Welsh at all, but the Anglo-Saxons' designation of their Celtic rivals, a special application of the word meaning "foreigners." About the Danes, later their enemies for two centuries, the English also felt strongly; yet the language of the Danes, being Germanic too, was obviously akin to English, and a great many more Danish words were borrowed than Celtic.

The attitude among the Old English, however, seems to have been on the whole linguistically conservative. Words for new things, new ways, and new knowledge that came in from abroad were quite as likely to be translated into Old English terms as to be directly borrowed. Though such words as *cirice* (church), *munuc* (monk), and *scrin* (shrine) were, it is true, borrowings or "loan-words," others such as *gōdspell* (gospel, literally "good-message") from Greek *euaggelion* (evangel), and *þrynnes* ("three-ness") from Latin *trinitas* (trinity), show clearly a part-by-part translation. Many others, too, show a sense-for-sense rendering into Old English terms: *elpendbān* (elephant-bone) for ivory, *palm-œppel* (palm-apple) for date, *leorning-cniht* (learning-youth) for disciple. . . .

As has already been said, though language is ever changing, change is restrained by a cultural or educational tradition, and accelerated by its absence or decay. In the prehistoric period (that is, before our earliest records begin in the seventh century) Old English underwent a considerable number of changes. Thanks to the personal interest and efforts of King Alfred the Great at the end of the ninth century, however, it attained for a while a measure of stability. . . .

The attacks of the Danes began, according to the *Chronicle*, in 787. By the time Alfred came to the throne a century later, they had won all of north and most of eastern England. Only the brilliant leadership of the young king saved the land—and the language; nor did the Danes win the throne till more than a hundred years after his death. Though the Danes began as pirates, ravaging the coasts and sailing away with their booty, they later settled and amalgamated with the English. Thus it is that their influence on the language was far more inward and homely than that of Norman French or of Latin, both of which were the languages of higher cultures dominating English, whereas the Scandinavian was more nearly on a par with the English. It does not appear, however, during the time of King Alfred.

Alfredian Old English shows us, very well preserved, the characteristics of a Germanic language. It was highly inflectional, distinguishing three numbers, three genders, and five cases, as well as three moods. In common with other Germanic languages it had lost the inflected passive voice, it distinguished only two tenses, and it had weak adjectives and weak verbs in addition to the strong. On looking at a passage of Old English, too, one notices at once that the word-order is frequently unlike the regular subject-verb-object order of Modern English; for in Old English the verb often precedes the subject (inverted order) or follows the object (transposed order).

The readiest way to summarize these first impressions of Old English is to analyze a typical passage of its prose. Here is a selection—part of Alfred's preface to his translation of *Pastoral Care*.

When I then	this all remembered,	then wondered I	exceedingly
Đā ic þā	ðis eall gemunde,	ðā wundrade ic	swīðe swīðe

of the good wise men	who formerly were	throughout
þāra gōdena wiotona	þe gīu wǣron	giond

England,	and the books	all	completely	learned	had,
Angelcynn,	ond þā bēc	ealla	be fullan	geliornod	hæfdon,

that they	of them	then	no	part	did not wish	into	their
þæt hīe	hiora	þā	nǣnne	dæl	noldon	on	hiora

own	language	to turn.	But I	then	soon	again	myself
āgen	geðiode	wendan.	Ac ic	þā	sona	eft	mē selfum

answered	and	said.	"They not	thought that	ever	men
andwyrde	ond	cwæð.	"Hīe ne	wēndon þætte	ǣfre	menn

should	so	reckless	become,	and the	learning	so
sceolden	swǣ	rēccelēase	weorðan,	ond sīo	lār	swǣ

fall away;	for the	desire (i.e., intentionally)	they it
oðfeallan;	for þǣre	wilnunga	hīe hit

neglected,	and	wished	that here	the more	wisdom	in (the)
forlēton,	ond	woldon	ðæt hēr	þȳ māra	wīsdom	on

land	should be	the	we more	languages	knew."
londe	wǣre	þȳ	wē mā	geðīoda	cūðon.". . .

With this glimpse of the language in its Old English stage, we may pass on to the developments in the Middle English period. As has been indicated, the transition from the one to the other was gradual; further, it is clear that it did not proceed at a uniform rate in all the dialects. In the north, changes were earlier and more rapid than in the south, so that by the year 1100, which we have taken as the dividing line, the northern dialect, even in its literary form, had already distinctly assumed the aspect of Middle English. The southern dialect changed more slowly, and in its literary form remained till at least 1150 essentially what we know as Old English.

What, then, are the changes which distinguish the new Middle English phase of the language from the Old English? All parts were affected, but the most fundamental difference was in the widespread "leveling" of inflectional endings, that is, a great reduction in their number and complexity. This simplification, and others such as the loss of "grammatical" gender in favor of "natural" gender and the increase in the use of normal word-order, had clearly begun before the Norman Conquest. It is therefore easy to overrate, as many have done, the immediate effects of this political and social upheaval upon the language. . . .

The Middle English period covers four centuries, however, during which time the enemies, Saxon and Norman, became gradually welded into a single nation with a single speech. If the immediate influence of the Normans on English was chiefly negative, it began within a century to be positive, and this appears very strikingly in the number of Norman French words, and later Parisian French, that English absorbed. The Old English word-stock was virtually unilingual: the Middle English became bilingual. . . .

The Middle English period, then, was one of transition, when a language already tending to lose its inflec-

tions was hastened in that process by political upset
and loss of prestige; when, its grammatical machinery
having been much simplified, it began to increase its
resources of vocabulary and idiom, chiefly under the
powerful influence of the French language; and finally
when, with Englishmen rising in the world who had
never abandoned their vernacular, and whose popular
support had to come from speakers of that same vernacular, the English language emerged once again, de-
posing its French rival.

Professor Baugh shows vividly, with dated citations,
how English becomes reinstated as French falls away,
particularly in the fourteenth century. In 1258 comes
the first royal proclamation to be made in English as
well as French. By the 80's of the same century many
voices of complaint are raised in the universities because the Fellows are speaking neither Latin nor
French, but English. By 1300, writers begin to use
French less because, they say, though some can still
understand it, everyone understands English. . . .

By the end of that century, with Geoffrey Chaucer,
English poetry reached a level which it was not to
achieve again before Elizabeth's day. Chaucer—as any
great literary artist does—saw for himself and made
abundantly clear to others the resources of the language in which he chose to work. We may do well to
look at a passage from the most English of his works,
and to see what the language had come to look like
in the five centuries since King Alfred:

> With hym ther was his sone, a yong Squier,
> A louyere and a lusty bacheler,
> With lokkes crulle, as they were leyd in presse.
> Of twenty yeer of age he was, I gesse;

Of his stature he was of euene lengthe
And wonderly delyuere and of greet strengthe;
And he hadde been sometyme in chyuachie
In Flaundres, in Artoys, and Pycardie,
And born hym weel, as of so litel space,
In hope to stonden in his lady grace.
Embrouded was he, as it were a meede
Al ful of fresshe floures whyte and reede;
Syngynge he was or floytynge al the day;
He was as fresh as is the monthe of May.
Short was his gowne with sleues long and wyde;
Wel koude he sitte on hors and faire ryde;
He koude songs make and wel endite,
Iuste and eek daunce and weel purtreye and write.
So hoote he loued that by nyghtertale
He sleep namoore than dooth a nyghtyngale.
Curteis he was, lowely and seruysable,
And carf biforn his fader at the table.

Perhaps the first thing that strikes us is the word-order—how much like that of Modern English it has become. Adjectives, it is true, are more often given prominence at the beginning of the line, with consequent inversion of the verb and subject: "Embrouded was he," "Short was his gowne"; but contrast "Syngynge he was." Except for a few words (and discounting the differences in spelling) the vocabulary is so familiar that it can be made out almost at sight. *Lusty*, *bacheler*, *euene*, and one or two other words have unfamiliar senses, and *delyuere*, *chyuachie*, *nyghtertale* are now obsolete; but these are decidedly in the minority. Excluding the proper names we find 23 different words of French origin: 12 nouns, 5 adjectives (including one participle), 5 verbs, and 1 adverb, all but two of which (*iuste* and *chyuachie*) are still in Modern English. Since there are, in the same passage, 52 different words of English origin in the same parts of speech (16 nouns, 13 adjectives, 15 verbs, and 8 adverbs), it is clear that in these categories the French element is close to one third of the total. However, the pronouns (22), articles (8), prepositions (20), conjunctions (24), and numerals (1), have remained almost exclusively English, and since they are the words most frequently repeated, they preserve the predominantly English cast of the language. Fewer and less complex inflections are found here than in Old English: in nouns in this passage we find the regular plural (*lokkes, floures*, and so on) and an old genitive (*lady*); in verbs we find the infinitive sometimes still inflected (*stonden*) but more often not (*sytte, ryde, make, write*). The auxiliary verbs and most of all the personal pronouns preserve the fuller inflection of Old English—as they still do in Modern English.

Not only did the fourteenth century see English firmly and finally established as a literary language, but it saw the elevation of one dialect into a commanding position. Hitherto there had been rival claimants among the three groups of dialects, Northern, Midland, and Southern. Beginning with the fourteenth century, however, a single subdivision of one of these, the East Midland dialect of the capital, the court, and the universities, assumed a peculiarly favored position as the literary standard, and it was never seriously threatened thereafter. . . .

The fifteenth century saw the standardization of the literary language carried further, though there were still occasional references to the fact that dialectal differences are a stumbling-block. Thus, Caxton, who was probably made more conscious of such difference through his long residence abroad, complained that "it is hard to please every man because of diversity and change of language." . . .

After this time, though alternate consolidation and expansion of the language continues, it is less violent, less revolutionary. One obvious reason is that never again was England subjected to foreign conquest. Nevertheless, in one sense something like this did happen: in the sixteenth century, the republic of letters was conquered by the humanistic movement, the revival of learning that put the study of Latin on a new basis and introduced the study of Greek. . . .

The general effect of the Renaissance in the progress of the English language was twofold: a temporary neglect of the vernacular by those whose classical studies made them almost contemptuous of modern tongues, but a later recognition of the possibility of giving to modern languages something of the grace and the sonorous quality that scholars found in the classics. In addition, the developing of nationalistic feeling under the later Tudors gave a new incentive to the literary use of the vernacular. The great tradition of Biblical translation, from Wiclif and Purvey in the fourteenth century through Tindale and Coverdale in the sixteenth, to the King James version of 1611, is likewise to be mentioned as one of the channels through which literary Modern English took form and exerted a powerful and widespread influence.

What is perhaps most striking in the attitude of scholars and writers toward the English language in the early Modern English period is a tendency to divide into two opposing camps: those who held that English should be "improved" by free importations from without, particularly by borrowings from Latin; and those who believed that the language should rather develop its own resources, and that an admixture of other languages meant not improvement but corruption. These points of view are, of course, signs of the opposite beliefs about vocabulary that have always existed and, to some extent, will always exist; but conservative and radical tendencies in this field have seldom been so consciously and definitely opposed as they were in the late sixteenth century. . . . The eventual victory was with the radical camp, and . . . in the Renaissance there was established, once and for all—though there are, to be sure, later qualifications—the principle of liberal word-borrowing as a permanent policy of the language. . . .

From the preceding article on the history of English, we have formed some idea of the tremendous wealth of synonyms which our language has gained from its borrowings from other languages. Yet this very richness of vocabulary can lead a careless writer into confusion, vagueness, and pretentiousness. Has all this borrowing resulted in profit or loss for our language? J. A. Sheard considers the problem here. He concludes that in skilled hands, English "is capable of a degree of precision and energy which can be equalled in few languages either ancient or modern."

J. A. SHEARD

Profit and Loss*

What of the position of the English vocabulary today? . . . One undeniable fact [is] the enormous increase in the vocabulary of English in the last fifteen

* Reprinted from *The Words We Use* by J. A. Sheard by permission of Andre Deutsch Limited. Copyright, 1954, by Andre Deutsch Limited.

hundred years. Our vocabulary is much richer than the vocabulary of, for example, two other leading languages, French and German, and this has arisen chiefly because English has been prepared to accept words from almost every language with which her people have come into contact. . . .

. . . We may indeed ask if mere number of words is in itself an advantage. . . . Words are useful only in so far as they can be used efficiently to express ideas. Our . . . task here is to see if, alongside the development in vocabulary, there has also been a development of the power of expression.

. . . There have been periods in the history of English when the feeling for purity of language has been strong. The Anglo-Saxons showed a strong preference for the native word, and, although Middle English preferred to borrow, there was a strong reaction to this attitude in the Renaissance period, when the purists opposed the introduction of 'inkhorn' terms. The linguistic licence of Elizabethan times was followed by a further reaction in favour of purity in the eighteenth century. There was a cult of Anglo-Saxon diction in the nineteenth century, and its followers tried to replace loan-words by native forms. The movement is not dead even today, for there are still teachers who drill their pupils in a blind preference for the Anglo-Saxon word, no matter how expressive its foreign synonym may be, or, more moderately, to prefer the native word, other things being equal. . . .

The general opinion is that English is better for all this borrowing, but whether this is so or not is difficult to determine. The answer can be found, if at all, only by an analysis of the powers of the language at different periods, in order to show . . . whether or not the language is better able to express new ideas as they arise. The starting point of such an analysis must obviously be Old English. . . . The language of the Anglo-Saxons . . . was fully equal to the demands they could reasonably make upon it. The vocabulary was sufficient for all the activities of life for which we have evidence, their love of fighting, admiration for personal bravery and prowess in battle, the simple emotions of a primitive people, the virtues and ideals of such a people, their social life, centered chiefly around the comitatus and fellowship in the hall. They were also well supplied with words describing the natural features of their country, and for the organization of the land on the simple lines which sufficed for them. If that were all it would perhaps be sufficient, yet we have already seen that when these people came into contact with quite unfamiliar ideas, as a result of the impact of Christianity and Mediterranean civilization upon a race hitherto heathen and barbarian, they were able to adapt their own language to express most of these ideas. We may, therefore, go a long way towards agreeing with Jespersen's opinion that, left to its own devices, the language might well have been able to cope with the new ideas as they presented themselves, just as German has done. . . .

Before discussing the question further, however, we ought to examine these loan-words to see if we can differentiate between them. . . .

. . . We should bear in mind that the earliest Latin, Scandinavian, and French words have been so well assimilated that they seem to be almost as English as the native words—for the ordinary man there is a great deal of difference between such words as *mile*, *ounce*, *law*, *face* and *beef* on the one hand, and *hypo-*

chondriac, orthodontics, and *schizophrenia* on the other—and often the early loans are as short, expressive, and convenient as the native words. There is, then, a difference between the two types of loan-words, and the position of the former group lies perhaps midway between that of the original native word and the easily-recognized loan-word of later times, so that there is perhaps not the wide gulf between native word and loan-word, the hard and fast division into two sharply-differentiated types, that might be expected. . . . Apart from actual origin, there is a good deal in common between some of the loan-words and our native words. . . .

Another point must also be borne in mind in discussing the effect of all this borrowing on our language. If we are to base our reasoning on a study of the forms recorded in the dictionary it is very easy to overestimate the effect of the foreign words. The actual number of native words in any of our large standard dictionaries is extremely small compared with the number of foreign borrowings recorded, and even if we were to confine our examination to those words in common use we should still find the native material outnumbered by about four to one. On the other hand, if we were to take a piece of English written on the popular level, or, better still, a passage of familiar conversation, we should find the proportions about reversed. It has been estimated that less than fifty words, all of them native words, suffice for more than half our needs, if we count every word used, including repetitions. . . . Emerson, quoting from George P. Marsh's *Lectures on the English Poets,* notes that, on such a count, Shakespeare has only ten per cent of borrowed words, Milton nineteen per cent, Johnson twenty-eight per cent, Gibbon thirty per cent, Tennyson twelve per cent, and the Bible (basing the count on three Gospels only) has no more than six per cent. We see, therefore, how important for all purposes is the comparatively small nucleus of native words.

Since the general opinion is that English has, in the main, benefited from the adoption of so many foreign loan-words, the advantages which have accrued from the use of these borrowings may be taken first, and the obvious one is the wealth of synonyms which have been created by the adoption of a foreign word—in some cases, words, from more than one foreign language—to express an idea for which English already had a word. Some of these are what we may call perfect synonyms, those in which it is very difficult to detect any difference at all in the meaning; others are not quite so exact, and there is some differentiation, though perhaps only in usage; a third group shows marked differences within the same basic idea, differences which arise from desynonymization, a process which we might expect to take place in any language which possesses several words for the same idea. . . . The result of this is extremely advantageous, for the language is thereby enabled to express subtle differences in the same thought. Sometimes the differentiation may go no further than the use of a particular word in one context and its approximate synonym in another; there is really no difference in the ideas expressed by *begin*, *commence*, and *start*, and yet the practised writer feels instinctively that one of these words 'belongs' in a particular passage, and that the other two could not be used there. Other pairs of this type, where the differentiation is one of usage rather than actual meaning, are *bloom* and *flower*, *buy* and *purchase*, *luck* and *fortune*, *work* and *labour*, the native word being here placed first in each case.

Sometimes the difference may be an emotional one, perhaps because the native word is closer to the spirit and tradition of the language. As a result of this the associations are deeper, simpler, and the word is more expressive, more powerful emotionally. There is often a coldness and aloofness about the borrowed word, even when it is used to express a feeling in which we might expect such qualities to be lacking. *Charity* is a fine word, and can be used with great effect, as in the famous passage in St. Paul's Epistle to the Corinthians, but it does not possess for us the warmth and friendliness of *love*. . . .

We may now consider examples, again confining ourselves to pairs comprising a native word and a loanword, in which there has been an appreciable divergence of meaning. If we use the adjective *boyish* of some action it implies rather approval, in a friendly manner, than condemnation, as when we refer to 'a boyish escapade,' something mischievous, but no more than that. If, however, we describe an action as *puerile* the attitude we have adopted towards it is a very different one. Although we shall, for the time being, confine ourselves to pairs of words, it may be noted here in passing that a third word, also a native word, *childish*, belongs in this group, again with a difference of meaning, and occupying a position midway between the others, not so derogatory as puerile, not so tolerant as boyish, and yet not having quite the sense of either. It would be a mere waste of time to give here a lengthy list of such pairs, for they spring at once to mind, yet a few may be quoted to illustrate the point: among pairs in very common use we may note *brotherly* and *fraternal, fatherly* and *paternal, hearty* and *cordial, heavenly* and *celestial, lively* and *vivacious, motherly* and *maternal, murder* and *homicide, shepherd* and *pastor, timely* and *temporal.* Sometimes we may extend the differentiation so as to include three or more words, such as *kingly, royal,* and *regal,* all expressing one basic idea, but each also expressing a different aspect of it. Among groups of four we may note *earthen, earthly,* and *earthy,* all from the native word, and all with different meanings, and also the loan-word *terrestial,* or we may compare the different senses of *male, manly, mannish,* and *masculine,* or *female, feminine, womanish,* and *womanly;* here we may note particularly the wide difference in meaning between the native words *manly* and *mannish, womanly* and *womanish.*

We have already noted that differentiation is not only between native word and loan-word; different senses, as we saw, developed from one root in *earthen, earthly,* and *earthy,* to take a native example, or *royal* and *regal,* to take loan-words. The last pair shows us another type of synonym, where the form of one word borrowed from a particular language may differ from that borrowed from the same root in the same language at a different time. *Ward* and *guard* are obviously connected in a sense, though their meanings are not identical today, and the difference in form arises from the fact that the words were borrowed from different French dialects at different times. *Warden* and *guardian* provide another example, but in the case of *warranty* and *guarantee* the divergence in meaning has not been so pronounced. French, as we have seen, is developed from Latin, so that if we borrow from both these languages we are in effect borrowing from one language at different periods; from the same root we have *royal*, adopted through French, and *regal*, borrowed directly from Latin, with a difference in form arising from borrowing at different periods, and also a distinct difference in meaning. In a similar case we may note three forms, *legal*, direct from Latin, *loyal*, through French, and the archaic and dialectal *leal*, also through French. . . .

There can be little doubt that the ability to express such fine shades of meaning is a distinct advantage, for the English writer who really knows his own language need never be at a loss for a word to express exactly what he means; *le mot juste* is, in most cases, available to him, and his thoughts can be expressed with the greatest precision. But there is a pitfall in this very advantage; the clear and accurate thinker will use his words well, but few attain to a complete control over both thought and language, and any loose and inaccurate thinking will inevitably be revealed by a faulty choice from the wealth of words available; either the clear distinctions will be lost in the writings of such a man, careless choice tending to blur the sharp lines dividing one sense from another, or the words may be used inaccurately, with a meaning or in a context not applicable to that particular word. There is, therefore, a disadvantage in the very richness of the vocabulary, for the greater the choice the greater the risk of error. . . .

Much of the richness of any language is due, of course, to the tendency of word meanings to radiate outward from the physical, concrete objects which a man touches to all the related experiences with which

he associates that object. Formerly special lecturer on Hispano-American literature at Harvard University and author of *Studies in Spanish-American Literature and Brazilian Literature*, Isaac Goldberg illustrates this principle of language growth in the following discussion of the word *hand*. He explains, too, why *dexterity* (from the Latin *dexter*, "right") and all the words related to the right side are considered "good" words, whereas *sinister* (from the Latin *sinister*, "left") and all the words related to the left side are considered "bad" words.

ISAAC GOLDBERG

Hand and Tongue*

. . . Between the hand and the tongue—between *manufacture* (doing things with the hands) and *language* (saying things with the tongue) man has built the entire structure of civilization.

The tool is an extension of the hand. The word becomes an extension of the mind, of the act.

It is natural, then, that the hand should figure largely in the human vocabulary, and that, like most words signifying concrete realities, it should lend itself to the most abstract combinations. The hand touches, it points, it makes, it counts. If it were not for touch, it is questionable that our sight would be able to appreciate fully the third dimension. We achieve "a feeling for form" by first *feeling form* in actuality.

To *manage* (Latin *manus*, 'hand') is to handle or to govern. To *maneuver* is originally to work with the hands. (Compare our words *handiwork* and *hand-*

* From: *The Wonder of Words* by Isaac Goldberg. Copyright, 1938, D. Appleton-Century Co., Inc. Reprinted by permission of the publishers Appleton-Century-Crofts, Inc.

work.) To be handy is to be dexterous. To *manipulate* meant, at first, to lead by the hands. When one receives a *mandate*, it means that something has been put into one's hands. *Handsome* itself at first meant dexterous.

To *command* and to *commend* are both linked, in origin, to *mandate* and therefore to Latin *manus*, 'hand.' To *commend* is originally to place in one's hands.

Verbs for grasping objects easily become verbs for grasping ideas. To *comprehend* is, indeed, first to seize. The monkey has a *prehensile* tail; man has a *prehensile* mind. "Do you understand?" is formal language; it has, as the verb still shows, a literal origin. Informally it is translated, "Do you *catch on?*"

To *capture* is to seize, physically; from the Latin *capere*, 'to seize,' 'to catch,' are derived likewise the final element in all our combinations such as *receive, perceive, conceive, accept*, and the middle element in such terms as *inception, reception, deception*. *Capire*, in Italian, is 'to understand'; it is derived from the selfsame Latin verb, *capere*. The German *begreifen*, 'to seize,' is also used for 'to understand.' We pick up information. We "hand it" on, or down. To *apprehend* is not only to catch but to learn (French, *apprendre*; Spanish, *aprender*).

Bechtel has shown that "words for sense perception in the Indo-European have only secondarily acquired this meaning, while primarily they designate the activity by which we perceive or the object which we perceive."

Thus, to *feel* is connected with hand (Greek, *palamē*).

Thus *dicere* itself (Latin, 'to say') originally meant

'to point.' We still say that a man *indicates*, or *points out*, what he means.

The testimony of language is clear: the beginning of understanding is in man's physical, sensual experience with the objects that surround him. . . .

Right- and Left-Handedness

That left portion of the brain which controls speech and other activity determines also, in a different area, the motions of the right half of the body. Our right hands generally are stronger than our left because the left side of the brain is generally more fully developed than the right. This has led to a human preference that is clearly mirrored in language.

Any child with a marked tendency toward left-handedness has learned, at the cost of discomfort and subtle outrage to his being, that the world is prejudiced in favor of right-handedness. Specialists in neurology and psychiatry share the belief that the regimentation of the left-handed child is attended by a violation of the nervous system, and is not to be undertaken lightly. We have been educated very slowly, it is true, away from the prejudice. The left-handed boy who used to be regarded, and therefore regarded himself, as an inferior creature, has lost some of his feeling after attending a baseball game and seeing in what high esteem the "southpaw" pitcher is held, as well as the special care with which the ball is pitched to left-handed batters.

The prejudice, however, is now fixed in language and will not, in all likelihood, ever be eradicated. The human bias in favor of the right hand arises from its greater dexterity. *Dexterity*, indeed, means right-handedness; *dexter*, Latin for 'right,' is akin to the

Sanskrit *daksh*, meaning 'to be strong.' Our word *left*, not strangely, comes from a Teutonic series meaning, generally, 'weak.'

The left hand, in most people, is the less skillful; few are ambidextrous, which is to say, if we translate literally, possessed of two right hands, just as we say of an awkward person that he is all thumbs. *Gawky* is akin to French *gauche*, which means 'left,' and, consequently, *awkward*. We all know what is meant by a left-handed compliment. Illegitimacy of offspring, whether in the symbols of heraldry or in popular speech, is designated by reference to the left hand. The bend sinister (inexactly called the bar sinister) is the heraldic emblem of bastardy. (Latin: *sinister*, 'left.') We call certain marriages left-handed because the groom gives his left, not his right, hand to the bride, in token of the fact that the marriage is morganatic—to one of inferior station, who does not acquire for herself or for her children the rights that would normally accrue to the wife and offspring of the husband. Such a wife and such offspring are commonly called left-handed. Ko-Ko, in *The Mikado*, relating the false execution of Nanki-Poo, speaks of baring his "good right arm." We refer to an invaluable assistant as our "right-hand man."

The right side, by a natural association of ideas, became the direction from which good omens came. The left, as naturally, became the side of sinister omens.

From the physical category the conception invades the mental and moral. A direct road is a straight road. *Direct* comes from the Latin *rectus*, akin to Sanskrit *rju*, 'straight,' 'right,' and to German *recht*, as well as to our own *right* and *correct*. So, in French, *droit* (Latin, *directus*) replaces *diestre*, from Latin *dextera*, and means 'right,' whether relating to the hand or to an idea; capitalize it and it becomes *Droit*, the 'Law'— the embodiment of that which is right in the eyes of society. Usually, that which is right is erected into orthodox belief. *Orthodoxy* comes from Greek *orthos,* 'right' (i.e., correct) and *doxia*, 'teaching.'

Thus the right hand, by various radiations of meaning, gives it name to skill, proper thinking, justice; the left symbolizes clumsiness, improper thought or deed, injustice. The wider the departure of a political party from conventional principles, the more it is held to move to the left. Originally, it moved actually to the left, for the more radical parties were seated to the left of the presiding officer. Such a seating, however, is itself a comment upon the left as a side of threatening omen.

Author of such books as *30 Days to a More Powerful Vocabulary* and *Six Weeks to Words of Power,* Wilfred Funk has for years contributed to the *Reader's Digest* the vocabulary feature "It Pays To Increase Your Word Power." In 1940 Funk established a publishing house in his own name; prior to that time he was president for fifteen years of Funk and Wagnalls, the firm founded by his father. Funk and Wagnalls publishes the Funk and Wagnalls Standard Dictionary Series.

In this excerpt from *Word Origins and Their Romantic Stories,* Funk tells the story of animal names. Like the words which Goldberg discusses for us, animal names, too, have come into English from other languages. Like the words in "Hand and Tongue," animal names, too, become bright and interesting once we really look at the word which daily habit has dulled.

Wilfred Funk

Where Animal Names Come From*

The wealth of our English language is almost beyond belief. Its prodigality can be dramatized if we
merely select a few of the words that are used to indicate the offspring of animals.

We speak, for instance, of the calf of a cow. But
the calf of a horse is a foal; the foal of a bear is a cub;
the cub of a beaver is a kitten; the kitten of a deer
is a fawn; the fawn of a sheep is a lamb; the lamb of a
dog is a pup; the pup of a goat is a kid; the kid of a
wolf is a whelp; and the whelp of a kangaroo is, of
all things, a joey.

The word *animal* originates in the Latin term *anima*
which means "breath." That is, an animal is an "ani-
mate" being, a thing that lives and breathes and moves,
unlike a plant which is incapable of rapid motor responses.

The histories that lie behind the names of animals
are usually simple and brief since their names most
often arise from their cries, their habits and characteristics, or from their place of origin.

Your *schnauzer* dog, for instance, that originated in
Germany at least 500 years ago is so named because
schnauzer is the German word for "growler." Your
gun dog, the *setter*, who now stands alert and rigid
when he is pointing, was once trained to crouch down
or "set" when game was scented, so his nickname is

* Reprinted from *Word Origins and Their Romantic Stories*, by
Wilfred Funk, by permission of the publishers, Wilfred Funk, Inc.,
N.Y.

obvious. Conversely the source of the name of that other gun dog, the *pointer*, can be easily guessed.

The big, shaggy *Newfoundland* came from the island of Newfoundland; the *Pomeranian* from Pomerania, a province in northeastern Prussia on the Baltic Sea; the tiny Pekingese is a Chinese pug named for the city of Peking; and the *Airedale* is from the valley or "dale" of the Aire in Yorkshire, England. In Old French the word *mestif* meant "mongrel" and this giant, smooth-haired chap inherited his name *mastiff* from this rather unattractive source. So, strictly speaking, the fearsome Hound of the Baskervilles was just a mutt.

The Germans raised the *boxer* breed of dogs for fighting and fighting is just what these square, short-haired dogs like to do better than anything else. Strangely enough they use their front paws in a fight pretty much like a pugilist, so their title *boxer* is a natural.

The French name for one of our popular dogs is *chien terrier*, or "earth dog." We call him a plain *terrier*, and the *terrier* part goes back eventually to the Latin *terra*, "earth." These dogs were supposed to dig up the earth and rout their quarry out of holes.

The *fox terrier* was used for hunting foxes. The *Kerry Blue* is from County Kerry, Ireland; the *Skye terrier* from Skye Island in Scotland; and the *Bedlington terrier* is named for a shire in Northumberland, England. This last dog may look like a lamb but he used to fight in a pit. The *bull terrier* is a mixture of the terrier and bull breeds.

When we think of a *bulldog* we are apt to have in mind the modern English bull with the smashed-in face. Old engravings show that the pit bull of that day actually had a long nose. The derivation of the term *bull* is not too sure, but many scholars believe that the dog received its title from bull-baiting, that sport in which dogs were set upon a bull in a fighting pit.

We have one proud and intelligent dog, a hunter and retriever type, whose known history goes back almost 2,000 years. This is the *poodle*. His name is straight from the German *Pudel*, short for *Pudelhund*. The *Pudel* part is from *pudeln* which means "splash in water," and *Hund* is "hound" or "dog." So our *poodle* is a "splash-hound" and the words *poodle* and *puddle* are from the same source.

Another dog of dignified history is the *St. Bernard*. He was named, as we know, after *St. Bernard* of Menthon, a great humanitarian of the 11th century who founded a hospice, or a house of refuge, at the pass of the great St. Bernard between Italy and Switzerland. Blizzards and avalanches made travel very perilous and the monks did much rescue work there with the aid of a breed of strong dogs. It was in this fashion that these *St. Bernard* dogs became famous for their intelligence and for the casks of brandy that they carried around their necks.

In this class there is that other dog of great strength and massive size, the smooth-coated *Great Dane*, who was once used to hunt the wild boar. He is named after the *Danes* of Denmark although he is supposed to be a German breed, centuries old in his lineage.

After these are three smaller numbers. First, the affectionate *dachshund*, the *Dachs* being German for "badger" which these dogs once hunted. Then there is the *spaniel* with his long, silky hair and pendulous ears. His name goes back through Old French *espagneul* to the Spanish *español*, which latter means just that— "Spanish." The initial "e" was lost along the way. The *cocker spaniel* earned his name because of the way he cocks his ears. And lastly there is that slow-moving hunting dog, the *basset hound* who has legs almost as short as the *dachshund*. The name *basset* fits the breed since in French *basset* means "very low."

And the *Scottie?* Well, no one has to be told that this is just a nickname for a little lad from Scotland. . . .

So far we have traced together the story of language from the cloudy prehistoric beginnings down through the ancient mother Indo-European, through the Germanic and Romance language families, and down to English, with its tremendously rich and complex heritage. Now we cross the Atlantic to certain remote colonies to see what changes took place in English when it was transplanted to America.

Everyone recalls the frequently quoted comment: "England and America are two countries separated by the same language." In this essay Louise Pound (formerly professor of English literature at the University of Nebraska, editor of many publications, and author of many studies in literature, linguistics, folklore, and educational subjects) characterizes our American English, pointing out how motion pictures, radio, and newspapers have helped to shape our rambunctious language. She discusses, too, the present attitude of the British toward the language whose rawness and impurity they once considered a serious threat to the King's English.

Louise Pound

American English Today*

Before the sixteenth century, that era of adventurous voyaging and world discovery, the English tongue had little interest for those dwelling outside of England. It was spoken in a foggy little island northwest of the European mainland, and the language of King Alfred, Chaucer, and Malory seemed of little importance to others. In the sixteenth century, the century of the Tudor monarchs and of Spenser and Shakespeare, began the colonizings that were to take English all over the world and to start up new centers of English civilization. One of these, founded along the Atlantic coast, was to develop into the United States of America. The speech of the daughter nation, too, was to have little interest for outsiders for a long period, unless to serve as an object of transatlantic disparagement. In the main, throughout the eighteenth and nineteenth centuries everything distinctively American in language was thought bad and modifications of British usage held to be corruptions. The mother tongue was authentic English and our new-world brand raw and impure, and the wise person would defer. Walt Whitman preached independence of old-world usage in language as well as in political ideas, and he sought to put some of his theories into practice. There were pioneer scholars, too, who fostered interest in American English in the nineties and later decades. Yet little more than a start was made. Even into the

* Reprinted from *Selected Writings of Louise Pound* by Louise Pound, by permission of University of Nebraska Press. Copyright 1949 by University of Nebraska Press.

early twentieth century it was emphasized by arbiters of style that it was English procedures that should prevail.

The World War with its shifts of emphasis and ferment of new ideas may be taken as the time of break between the old and the new attitudes. The tide of events following 1914, changing the calm and optimistic pre-War world into a time of intense strain and excitement, turned attention to things American all over the world. The experiences of these years heightened interest in American institutions, traditions, and history. There arose new interest in American literature. The popularity of this subject at educational institutions increased amazingly. There sprang up also interest in our national variety of the English speech, its beginnings, its relation to the mother tongue, its expansions of vocabulary, the New-World tendencies of the language. . . .

Now, after the World War, we are again in a period of freedom and change, with condensation and simplification and informality *desiderata*. The conventionalizing influence of schools, of teaching, of grammars and dictionaries is stronger than ever before, and the departures that appear may not seem very radical. They testify, however, to our reaction from authority and desire to shake off trammels. . . .

A complaint sometimes heard about present-day prose is that the sentence is disintegrating. In the desire for terseness and for realism there are abrupt stoppages in the expression of thought, or the thought is left unfinished. There are grammatical intercalations, and omissions of intermediate steps. All this may help to save space, and without cost of intelligibility, but it comes at the expense of beauty and completeness. The influence of the newspaper account, especially of its telegraphic headlines directed at the hurried reader, is stronger than love of the old fastidiousness and symmetry. . . .

Headlines have to be thought out rapidly, fitted to one column, and made to extend from one to four lines. The number of letters in a word is governed by the size of the type. No word may be divided at the end of a line and no word may be repeated. Every headline should have a verb expressed or implied, though none may begin with a verb. Therefore short forceful words must be depended upon. As a result of this quest for short cuts a standardized vocabulary has developed. "Zep Due to Sail on Tour of Orb," "Tell Tale Oil on Sea Spikes Hope for Lost Clipper," "Stenog Asks Heart Balm" are quite typical. . . .

Other phenomena of vocabulary concern word-forms themselves. The delight of the Elizabethans in playing with words has reappeared but without the Elizabethan greatness of expression. We miss the sixteenth-century sense of beauty. Our devotion is not to the beautiful but to the arresting, to colloquialisms, to slang, to doing strange things with words. . . . Audacities thrive; verbal license is unbridled. This is well illustrated by the language of periodicals like. . . . *Time* with its "cinemaudiences," "ballyhooligans," "intelligentsiacs," and by the vast journalistic literature telling of sound films. After O. Henry and his successors, unconventionalities became a cult, not however, unconventionalities of the spelling or dialect type relied on in the decades of Josh Billings and Artemus Ward. In their day it was rusticity that had humorous appeal. Newspaper columnists and writers for the stage and the films try, in our time, for linguistic stunts. Literary selectiveness in speech is left to the clergyman, the professor, and the old-fashioned.

It is a commonplace to remark how expressions once carefully avoided are now sought for. Witness the recurrence of what were long thought vulgarisms. Words once barred in polite conversation are pushed into the foreground. Slang, characterized in the first half of last century as "low" and "disgusting" language, now thrives despite the disapproval of purists and of the classroom. . . .

Blending, conscious or unconscious, is an old language process, like punning, which is often a type of blending; but never before was it in such conscious vogue. *Smog* for smoke and fog is now an official term of the weather bureau at Washington. The English college term *brunch* for food between breakfast and lunch has increasing currency in this country. Robert Benchley's "mirthquake," *After 1903—What?* was advertised in the New York *Times* as *colossapendous, stupificent, magnossal.* . . .

In the use of affixes there is no less freedom, for they are attached and interchanged at caprice. New formations appear unchecked. After the advent of *suffragette*, journalese gave the world *slackerette, huskerette, hoboette.* For a while the suffix of feminine names such as Christine, Josephine when utilized in *doctorine, actorine, batherine* aroused amusement, but only *chorine* has lingered. . . .

In some instances the vogue of an affix has come in the wake of a war. After the Cuban war *-o* was liked for a time, as in *Excello* shirts, *Indestructo* trunks, and *El Tosto* and *El Perco*, electric devices for toasting and percolating. It still flourishes, although *-co* from company (*Delco, Texaco*) is now more popular. After the Russo-Japanese war -*ski* as in the once current *allrightsky, et al.,* had its day, but it remains only in the useful *buttinski.* After the World War, the German -*fest* of *songfest, sobfest, swatfest, pepfest* came to the forefront, and it has proved the most lasting and prolific of the imported suffixes. . . .

It is time to revert from contemporary phenomena of the literary and subliterary language to the present status of American English. . . .

The English Conference held in London in 1927 discussed the feasibility of taking measures to keep together the diverging brands of English. . . .

Some Britons did not welcome it. Witness the following passage, quoted from the *New Statesman* of June 25, 1927, and signed with the initials W. W. . . .

We must hope that the forthcoming dicta [that of an international Committee] of this precious fifty-fifty Council will be received with precisely the respect they are likely to deserve—which is to say none at all. Taking the scheme as a whole, it is hard to say how its sheer fatuity could be surpassed. It is extremely desirable, to say the least, that every necessary effort should be made to preserve some standard of pure idiomatic English. But from what quarter is the preservation of such a standard in any way threatened? The answer is "Solely from America." Yet we are asked to collaborate with Americans on the problem; we are to make bargains about our own tongue; there is to be a system of give and take. Is it conceivable that any really living literary language could ever be "developed" on such lines? Why should we offer to discuss the subject at all with America? We do not want to interfere with their language; why should they seek to interfere with ours? That their huge hybrid population of which only a small minority are even racially Anglo-Saxon should use English as their chief means of intercommunication is our misfortune, not our fault. They certainly threaten our language, but the only way in which we can effectively meet that threat is by assuming—in the words of the authors of the King's English—that "Americanisms are foreign words and should be so treated." In any compromise between the King's English and the President's English there can be no imaginable advantage. . . . So bad cess to this new "Council" and all its works.

A fear of parental contamination through the introduction of Americanisms has often been expressed. . . . Some Britons, on the other hand, like Virginia Woolf in a passage often quoted, have rather welcomed importations from us: "When we want to freshen our speech we borrow from America—poppycock, rambunctious, booster, good mixer (ugly vigorous slang which creeps into use among us, first in talk, later in writing) come from across the water."

Of course England sends words to America too, though perhaps fewer than she imports. English slang comes quickly to this country *via* fiction and the stage. The humorist, P. G. Wodehouse, who is well versed in the slang of both countries, has probably done more than any other person to promote an interchange. But no one in the United States seems disturbed by the borrowings. We adopt *gadget, cheerio, my word, swank, goofy* and think nothing of it. And of course the staple fundamental language is hardly affected by transient popular colloquialisms anyway. Where the ideas to be expressed are trivial or facetious, the two vernaculars vary widely. Thus the slang of England and that of the United States are far from identical. When the subject matter is purely practical or commonplace, there is also much divergence. Travelers in London and shoppers generally really need glossaries of terms. But when the subject matter is of highest quality, is concerned with abstract values or fundamental concepts, the divergence is so slight as to be almost negligible.

There have been no more linguistic conferences since that in London in 1927. The prevention of divergence appeared to those in attendance difficult if not impossible, however unwelcome divergence might be, and this for several reasons. Retarding by fiat seemed out of the question. . . . Imagine a one-hundred-per-cent patriot, a member of the American Legion, coerced in the use of his mother tongue by the example of a Briton. Or a Briton coerced into American usage. The best that could be done would be to cultivate a sentiment of responsibility, a wish to hold together, to preserve. An attempt to have a fixed international form of cultivated usage, a "standard dialect" of English, one and one only right way of speaking, would have little chance of success.

Today times have changed, however, and we are now somewhat less fearful of divergence. In the last decade the English of England and the English of the United States have actually come closer together. Practical matters can help where the scholarly world cannot. Linkage through the telephone, the radio, and sound films has made a difference. There must be compromise if the largest number of people are to be reached by the new mechanical devices. Contrast the attitude of the *New Statesman* in 1927 with that of Lloyd James, linguistic adviser to the British Broadcasting Corporation, who, if newspaper reports may be relied on, recommended early in 1938 that the Corporation radio talkers copy the diction of President Franklin Roosevelt. Such recognition of a transatlantic model would have been out of the question in the old days. . . .

Whether one likes it or not, one cannot now minimize the influence of Hollywood. Films are made there, and California pronunciation, which neither diphthongizes o's, uses the "broad *a*," or drops final *r*, looms larger now than the pronunciation of Boston, once so admired. American pronunciation in general, like that of Ireland, Scotland, and Northern England, is less radical than that of Southern England, and it is actually more intelligible to hearers than so-called Public School or Received English. . . .

Some, in a wish to disparage it, call the English of America "old-fashioned"; others prefer to think of it as more historic, for it preserves older vowel sounds and middle syllables and is in some respects closer to the speech of Shakespeare, the King James Bible, and Milton than is London English. Hollywood diction, such as it is, seems to have increased the prestige of our national vernacular throughout the world.

English has everywhere outdistanced as the language most useful to travelers its former European rival, French. If it continues to gain in world standing, which brand of it is likelier to prevail, British or American?

Americans may be glad to know that the potentialities of their speech are now recognized overseas, yet no one in this country wishes New-World English to supplant British English in England itself. Thinking people welcome the present tendency toward compromise and minimizing. Though there are and must be divergences, it is to be hoped that they will remain minor shadings rather than fundamental differentiations. Whatever the future holds for the English language, on ancestral soil, on colonial soil, or on adopted soil, severance cannot be contemplated with enthusiasm. The gain of keeping diverging brands of English

speech fairly close together is too great to be yielded
sooner than is inevitable.

> Do you fry your eggs in a skillet, a frying pan, or a
> spider? Do you say "I have drunk" or "I have drank"?
> Do you pronounce *can, can* or *kin*? (It seems that an
> old lady in North Carolina once said of a crop of to-
> matoes, "Oh, we'll eat what we *kin*, and what we
> *cain't* we'll *can*.")
> Imagine a map of the United States showing where
> eggs are fried in a skillet, a frying pan, or a spider.
> Imagine a series of volumes of thousands of maps show-
> ing regional speech differences in vocabulary, grammar,
> and pronunciation. Gledhill Cameron, frequent con-
> tributor to *Collier's*, reports some of the findings of re-
> search interviewers who are at work throughout the
> United States gathering information on local speech
> differences for a colossal *Linguistic Atlas of the United
> States and Canada*.

GLEDHILL CAMERON

Some Words Stop at Marietta, Ohio*

What language do you speak? Would you call it
"plain American"? If so, you may be surprised to learn
that despite the vast influence of radio, TV, the mov-
ies, magazines, books and national advertising, many
of the words and expressions you use every day might
not even be understood by people elsewhere in the
United States—who also speak "plain American."

If you're a housewife, do you make bacon and eggs
in a frying pan—or, as many other American women

* Reprinted from "Some Words Stop at Marietta, Ohio," by
Gledhill Cameron, in *Collier's*, June 25, 1954, by permission of the
author.

do, in a *spider*, *creeper*, or *drip-drop*? When you clean house, do you *straighten up* or *tidy up*; *rid up* or *redd up* (as women do in some parts of New England, Ohio and Indiana); *make ménage* (as in New Orleans), or *muck out* (as in some Colorado mining communities)?

If Junior sneaks away from school, do your neighbors say he *skips*, *bags* or *lays out* of school, or that he *plays hooky* or *hooks Jack*? When he reports on how he spent his time, does he tell you he climbed trees, or that he *clim*, *clum*, *clome*, *cloom*, *clam*, or *clammed* them? If he ate too many green apples, does he get sick *to*, *at*, *in*, *with*, or *about* his stomach?

To chart the differences in vocabulary, grammar and pronunciation from one American community to another, a small band of language experts—professors and graduate students representing a number of universities—has been traveling around the country for the last 20 years, asking people what words they use for all sorts of simple, everyday objects and actions. They have compiled long lists of variants for everything from the words for the clavicles of a chicken (*wishbone*, *witch bone*, *pull bone*, *pully bone*, *lucky bone*, *merrythought*) to our expressions for the woman who's going to have a baby (she might be *in health*, *in the family way*, *in preggety*, *on the road to Boston*, *fragrant* or *footbroke*—the last a local Southern expression derived from an African word).

Sometimes the linguistic geographers use tape or disc recordings, but most of their minutely detailed data are collected in thousands of bulky notebooks, in a special phonetic script which can reproduce about 400 differences in vowel sounds alone. Using this script, the interviewers write down the casual conversations of men and women all over America exactly as they talk on their own front porches (*stoops, piazzas, galleries*). . . .

The information so exhaustively collected is going into a colossal work titled Linguistic Atlas of the United States and Canada (Canada is included to cover colloquial expressions which ignore the international boundary). When the atlas is finished, an estimated 10 years from now, it will contain thousands of maps showing local and regional speech differences and the geographical boundaries, called isoglosses, that limit the areas in which the words and expressions are used. The work is being done under the direction of the University of Michigan's Dr. Hans Kurath—an internationally known linguist who has been a leader of the atlas project since its origin in 1929.

The atlas actually will consist of a series of regional sets, the first of which, Linguistic Atlas of New England, already has been published. Its six volumes (price for the set: $185) were brought out by Brown University and the American Council of Learned Societies from 1939 to 1943, at a cost of about $250,000. Additional atlases are in various stages of completion, two at the University of Michigan, and others at the Universities of Minnesota, Colorado, New Mexico and California, the University of Washington at Seattle and Louisiana State University. Preliminary studies have been made for still another at the University of Texas.

Three kinds of map are used by the researchers to plot variations. First there's the lexical map, which shows the different words Americans use to indicate the same object or action. For example, "something extra" is *lagniappe* in New Orleans, something *to boot* in Kentucky, a *brawtus* in Charleston, South Carolina, a *pillon* in New Mexico—all good American words.

The linguists use a second, phonetic map to show differences in the pronunciation of the same words. The classic example is provided by the old lady in North Carolina who said about her crop of tomatoes, "Oh, we'll eat what we *kin,* and what we *cain't* we'll *can.*"

The morphological map, the third type, indicates differences in grammar. Widespread education is rapidly wiping out grammatical variations, the linguists have found. One Georgia man summed up the changes that are occurring: "I used to say, 'I drink water' and 'I have drinked,' " he proudly told an atlas fieldworker. "Now I say, 'I drink,' 'I drank' and 'I have drank.' "

Most of the regional departures from the common language of Americans (technically, we all speak what linguists call American English) involve the homey aspects of life: family relationships, kitchens and cookery, farm work, daily chores, children's play and other activities which are relatively immune from outside influences. Some of these localisms are confined to very small geographic areas, says Dr. Kurath. If you say *hook Jack,* meaning to be absent from school without leave, you are most probably from Cape Cod. If you call cows by hollering *chay!,* you're from Williamsburg County, South Carolina. If you're an old-timer from eastern Long Island, you might call a barnyard or cowpen a *pightle* (it rhymes with "title"). . . .

Judging from research to date, it's only in Indiana that a child coasting down a hill on a sled or wagon goes *bellity-bump*; and only around New London that he goes *belly-kuhchunk!* In the upper Midwest he may go downhill *boy fashion* and in Louisiana he'll go *scooting* or *head fo'most.* In other parts of the country he may go *belly flop, gut, bunt, bump, bumpus, button, bust, booster, wop, whack, womp, slide, slam, kuhchug,* or *grinder.*

The rural areas retain some of the most colorful speech localisms. In some sparsely settled parts of Maine, for example, you might still hear of a *gorming* (stupid) man who gets *all of a biver* (excited) about a *ding-clicker* (a pretty young woman) and invites her to a *hog-wrestle* (a dance). But he wouldn't propose until he was sure she wasn't *pizen neat* (too neat) or a *drozzle tail* (slovenly person). . . .

In *The Story of Language* Mario Pei makes this observation: ". . . when people migrate from their homeland, they are more likely to keep intact the language of the period of migration than do those who stay behind. The English of the Appalachian mountaineers is closer to seventeenth-century English than any present-day English dialect; the French of Canada is closer to seventeenth-century French than is the Parisian of today; Yiddish is closer to fifteenth century German than is present-day German; while the Portuguese of Brazil reflects the pronunciation of the period of discovery and colonization better than Lisbonese."

In the following article, V. Randolph and G. P. Wilson show that many Ozark expressions commonly thought of as "bad English" are in reality Elizabethan survivals which have lived on from past centuries in the isolated language island of the Ozark Mountains. (Vance Randolph is the author of *The Ozarks, An American Survival of Primitive Society; Ozark Folksongs;* and *We Always Lie to Strangers—Tall Tales from the Ozarks.*

G. P. Wilson is professor of English at Women's College, University of North Carolina, and is active in folklore societies.)

V. RANDOLPH AND G. P. WILSON

Survivals of Early English*

People from the cities are often struck with certain archaic words and phrases used by the hillfolk. . . . Expressions which seem odd to the overcultured may be and often are survivals of English used three centuries ago.[1]

Our common word *varmint*, for example, is derived from vermin, and preserves an older British pronunciation still standard in such English words as derby and clerk and even in the American pronunciation of sergeant. Surely the hillman's pronunciation of wrestle —he makes it sound like *wrastle*—has much in common with Chaucer's *wrastelying* and *wrastleth*.[2]

The preterite of eat is usually *et* in the Ozarks, a pronunciation still common among educated Englishmen, which is defended by the *Oxford Dictionary* and nearly all of the better dictionaries except Webster's, which gives the pronunciation as *āt* and adds, "in England usually *ĕt*." *The Dictionary of Modern English Usage* says, "The past is spelt *ate* and pronounced *ĕt* (wrongly *āt*)." In the Ozarks the past participle of eat is often pronounced *ĕt*, exactly like the preterite. This is true not only in Missouri and Arkansas, but also in eastern Oklahoma, according to the official guidebook

* Reprinted from *Down in the Holler: A Gallery of Ozark Folk Speech*, by Vance Randolph and George P. Wilson. Copyright 1953 by University of Oklahoma Press. Used by permission.

[1] *Missouri Magazine*, December, 1928, pp. 7, 25.

[2] *Canterbury Tales*, 15, 151; Third, 2, 863.

issued by the University of Oklahoma Press.[3] I don't think I ever heard a real old-timer Ozarker use the word *eaten*. The form *et* as a participle has been good English since 1300, and was used by Shakespeare, Fletcher, Fuller, Evelyn, Marvell, Purchas, Arbuthnot, Pope, Malmesbury, Peter Pindar, Dr. Johnson, Prior, Coleridge, Jane Austen, Dickens, Tennyson, Thackeray, and a host of other writers.

Chew, both noun and verb, is always *chaw* to the Ozarker, just as it was to Pepys[4] and Spenser,[5] a form almost universal in England in the seventeenth century, and still common in several English country dialects.

Dr. Samuel Johnson pronounced the preterite of hear with a long *e* sound, as did many Englishmen of his day.[6] Noah Webster always contended that heard was pronounced *heerd* until the beginning of the American Revolution, and argued that deaf should rhyme with leaf, just as it does today in Westmoreland, Cumberland, and some other parts of England.[7] Both *heerd* and *deef* are still very common pronunciations in the Ozark country.

Even the Ozark pronunciation of pert—we always call it *peert*—is descended from an older standard English pronunciation. Poor is invariably *pore* in the hill country, as it was in seventeenth-century England. *Slick* for sleek was used by Beaumont and Fletcher[8] exactly as it is in the Ozarks today.

In ordinary conversation the Ozarker addresses

[3] *Oklahoma, a Guide to the Sooner State,* 121.
[4] *Diary,* June 7, 1665.
[5] *Faërie Queene,* 2, 4, 30.
[6] Boswell's *Johnson* (1777), III, 369.
[7] Schele De Vere, *Americanisms* (New York, 1872), 462.
[8] *Knight of the Burning Pestle,* Act II, scene 1.

a married woman as *Miz* or *Mis'*, but in formal speeches, such as funeral sermons, he pronounces the word *Mistress* very distinctly, as the Elizabethans did. A backwoods preacher always referred to his wife as "my mistress"; he was horrified and incredulous when I told him that, to many Americans, the use of this word meant that there was no legal marriage between them. . . .

The disyllabic plurals ending in *es* so common in the Ozarks—*nestes, postes, deskes,* and the like—are survivals, too, which were still heard in nineteenth-century England. *Folkses* is probably a later formation on the same model. . . .

The hillman uses *bum* and *bummy* to mean buttocks,[9] and Logan Clendening reports that *bummy* is common in Virginia also.[10] *Bum* is heard in Warwickshire slang to this day, and Shakespeare used it with the same meaning.[11] Dr. Clendening quotes an old English jingle:

> Men run to belly and women to bum. . . .
> When to the age of forty they come,

"This here sugar-liquor ain't no good," said one of my neighbors at Pineville, Missouri, denouncing the synthetic "bourbon" sold in Kansas City. "You cain't make whiskey *withouten* corn." This is an old form of the preposition used by many early writers. Laurence Minot, about 1350, wrote a ballad praising King Edward II with the line: "And grante him joy withouten strife."

Many other words and phrases, denounced as "bad

[9] *American Speech,* Vol. XI (1936), 314.
[10] *The Human Body* (New York, 1927), 187.
[11] *A Midsummer Night's Dream,* Act II, scene 1, line 53.

English" by the schoolmasters, are of similar ancient lineage. . . . In the present work the intention is merely to show enough of the earlier usage to arouse interest in this aspect of the Ozark speech and stimulate further research on the part of the inquisitive.

Misuses and Abuses

What is happening to our language? Some of our critics concern themselves largely with the ignorant or careless misuse of language which results in empty absurdities; other critics are more concerned with the skillful abuse of language which makes it a dangerous tool with which to deceive and exploit human beings.

In the following section several perceptive writers present horrifying examples of what we must *not* do to our language. By implication, they define for us what clear, careful, honest writing is.

George Orwell, English essayist and novelist, numbers among his books *Nineteen Eighty-Four, Animal Farm, Burmese Days,* and *Homage to Catalonia.*

Concerned with the decline of language, he analyzes in the following essay five passages which exemplify the staleness of imagery and the lack of precision which he deplores. "Modern writing at its worst," he says, "does not consist in picking out words for the sake of their meaning and inventing images in order to make the meaning clearer. It consists in gumming together long strips of words which have already been set in order by someone else, and making the results presentable by sheer humbug."

He formulates five rules for writing clear, honest, in-

telligible prose, for if you write simple English, he says,
". . . when you make a stupid remark its stupidity will
be obvious, even to yourself."

Of course, what Orwell is primarily interested in is
exposing the comfortable, lying political euphemism
which masks the human facts of war, suffering, and
death. It is for this reason that Orwell feels so strongly
that we must work to make language simple and honest.

GEORGE ORWELL

Politics and the English Language*

Most people who bother with the matter at all
would admit that the English language is in a bad way,
but it is generally assumed that we cannot by conscious
action do anything about it. Our civilization is deca-
dent and our language—so the argument runs—must
inevitably share in the general collapse. It follows that
any struggle against the abuse of language is a sentimental archaism, like preferring candles to electric light
or hansom cabs to aeroplanes. Underneath this lies the
half-conscious belief that language is a natural growth
and not an instrument which we shape for our own
purposes.

Now, it is clear that the decline of a language must
ultimately have political and economic causes: it is
not due simply to the bad influence of this or that individual writer. But an effect can become a cause, re-
inforcing the original cause and producing the same
effect in an intensified form, and so on indefinitely. A
man may take to drink because he feels himself to be
a failure, and then fail all the more completely because

* From *Shooting an Elephant* by George Orwell. Copyright,
1945, 1946, 1949, 1950, by Sonia Brownell Orwell. Reprinted by
permission of Harcourt, Brace and Company, Inc.

he drinks. It is rather the same thing that is happening to the English language. It becomes ugly and inaccurate because our thoughts are foolish, but the slovenliness of our language makes it easier for us to have foolish thoughts. The point is that the process is reversible. Modern English, especially written English, is full of bad habits which spread by imitation and which can be avoided if one is willing to take the necessary trouble. If one gets rid of these habits one can think more clearly, and to think clearly is a necessary first step towards political regeneration: so that the fight against bad English is not frivolous and is not the exclusive concern of professional writers. I will come back to this presently, and I hope that by that time the meaning of what I have said here will have become clearer. Meanwhile, here are five specimens of the English language as it is now habitually written.

These five passages have not been picked out because they are especially bad—I could have quoted far worse if I had chosen—but because they illustrate various of the mental vices from which we now suffer. They are a little below the average, but are fairly representative samples. I number them so that I can refer back to them when necessary:

(1) I am not, indeed, sure whether it is not true to say that the Milton who once seemed not unlike a seventeenth-century Shelley had not become, out of an experience ever more bitter in each year, more alien [sic] to the founder of that Jesuit sect which nothing could induce him to tolerate.

Professor Harold Laski
(Essay in Freedom of Expression).

(2) Above all, we cannot play ducks and drakes with a native battery of idioms which prescribes such egregious

collocations of vocables as the Basic *put up with* for *tolerate* or *put at a loss* for *bewilder*.

Professor Lancelot Hogben
(*Interglossa*).

(3) On the one side we have the free personality: by
definition it is not neurotic, for it has neither conflict nor
dreams. Its desires, such as they are, are transparent, for
they are just what institutional approval keeps in the forefront of consciousness; another institutional pattern would
alter their number and intensity; there is little in them
that is natural, irreducible, or culturally dangerous. But *on
the other side*, the social bond itself is nothing but the
mutual reflection of these self-secure integrities. Recall the
definition of love. Is not this the very picture of a small
academic? Where is there a place in this hall of mirrors for
either personality or fraternity?

Essay on psychology in *Politics* (New York).

(4) All the "best people" from the gentlemen's clubs,
and all the frantic fascist captains, united in common
hatred of Socialism and bestial horror of the rising tide of
the mass revolutionary movement, have turned to acts of
provocation, to foul incendiarism, to medieval legends
of poisoned wells, to legalize their own destruction of
proletarian organizations, and rouse the agitated petty-
bourgeoisie to chauvinistic fervor on behalf of the fight
against the revolutionary way out of the crisis.

Communist pamphlet.

(5) If a new spirit *is* to be infused into this old country,
there is one thorny and contentious reform which must be
tackled, and that is the humanization and galvanization of
the B.B.C. Timidity here will bespeak canker and atrophy
of the soul. The heart of Britain may be sound and of
strong beat, for instance, but the British lion's roar at present is like that of Bottom in Shakespeare's *Midsummer
Night's Dream*—as gentle as any sucking dove. A virile
new Britain cannot continue indefinitely to be traduced
in the eyes, or rather ears, of the world by the effete lan-

guors of Langham Place, brazenly masquerading as "standard English." When the Voice of Britain is heard at nine
o'clock, better far and infinitely less ludicrous to hear
aitches honestly dropped than the present priggish, in-
flated, inhibited, school-ma'amish arch braying of blame-
less bashful mewing maidens!

Letter in *Tribune*.

Each of these passages has faults of its own, but,
quite apart from avoidable ugliness, two qualities are
common to all of them. The first is staleness of imagery; the other is lack of precision. The writer either
has a meaning and cannot express it, or he inadvert-
ently says something else, or he is almost indifferent
as to whether his words mean anything or not. This
mixture of vagueness and sheer incompetence is the
most marked characteristic of modern English prose,
and especially of any kind of political writing. As soon
as certain topics are raised, the concrete melts into the
abstract and no one seems able to think of turns of
speech that are not hackneyed: prose consists less and
less of *words* chosen for the sake of their meaning,
and more and more of *phrases* tacked together like the
sections of a prefabricated hen-house. I list below,
with notes and examples, various of the tricks by
means of which the work of prose-construction is habitually dodged:

Dying metaphors. A newly invented metaphor as-
sists thought by evoking a visual image, while on the
other hand a metaphor which is technically "dead"
(e.g. *iron resolution*) has in effect reverted to being an
ordinary word and can generally be used without loss
of vividness. But in between these two classes there
is a huge dump of worn-out metaphors which have
lost all evocative power and are merely used because

they save people the trouble of inventing phrases for themselves. Examples are: *Ring the changes on, take up the cudgels for, toe the line, ride rough-shod over, stand shoulder to shoulder with, play into the hands of, no axe to grind, grist to the mill, fishing in troubled waters, on the order of the day, Achilles' heel, swan song, hotbed.* Many of these are used without knowledge of their meaning (what is a "rift," for instance?), and incompatible metaphors are frequently mixed, a sure sign that the writer is not interested in what he is saying. Some metaphors now current have been twisted out of their original meaning without those who use them even being aware of the fact. For example, *toe the line* is sometimes written *tow the line.* Another example is *the hammer and the anvil,* now always used with the implication that the anvil gets the worst of it. In real life it is always the anvil that breaks the hammer, never the other way about: a writer who stopped to think what he was saying would be aware of this, and would avoid perverting the original phrase.

Operators or *verbal false limbs.* These save the trouble of picking out appropriate verbs and nouns, and at the same time pad each sentence with extra syllables which give it an appearance of symmetry. Characteristic phrases are *render inoperative, militate against, make contact with, be subjected to, give rise to, give grounds for, have the effect of, play a leading part (role) in, make itself felt, take effect, exhibit a tendency to, serve the purpose of, etc., etc.* The keynote is the elimination of simple verbs. Instead of being a single word, such as *break, stop, spoil, mend, kill,* a verb becomes a *phrase,* made up of a noun or adjective tacked on to some general-purposes verb such as *prove, serve, form, play, render.* In addition, the passive voice is wherever possible used in preference to the active, and noun constructions are used instead of gerunds (by *examination of* instead of *by examining*). The range of verbs is further cut down by means of the *-ize* and *de-* formations, and the banal statements are given an appearance of profundity by means of the *not un-*formation. Simple conjunctions and prepositions are replaced by such phrases as *with respect to, having regard to, the fact that, by dint of, in view of, in the interests of, on the hypothesis that;* and the ends of sentences are saved from anticlimax by such resounding commonplaces as *greatly to be desired, cannot be left out of account, a development to be expected in the near future, deserving of serious consideration, brought to a satisfactory conclusion,* and so on and so forth.

Pretentious diction. Words like *phenomenon, element, individual* (as noun), *objective, categorical, effective, virtual, basic, primary, promote, constitute, exhibit, exploit, utilize, eliminate, liquidate,* are used to dress up simple statement and give an air of scientific impartiality to biased judgments. Adjectives like *epoch-making, epic, historic, unforgettable, triumphant, age-old, inevitable, inexorable, veritable,* are used to dignify the sordid processes of international politics, while writing that aims at glorifying war usually takes on an archaic color, its characteristic words being: *realm, throne, chariot, mailed fist, trident, sword, shield, buckler, banner, jackboot, clarion.* Foreign words and expressions such as *cul de sac, ancien régime, deus ex machina, mutatis mutandis, status quo, gleichschaltung, weltanschauung,* are used to give an air of culture and elegance. Except for the useful abbreviations *i.e., e.g.,* and *etc.,* there is no real need for any of the hundreds of foreign phrases now current in English. Bad writers, and especially scientific, political and sociological writers, are nearly always haunted by the notion that Latin or Greek words are grander than Saxon ones, and unnecessary words like *expedite, ameliorate, predict, extraneous, deracinated, clandestine, subaqueous* and hundreds of others constantly gain ground from their Anglo-Saxon opposite numbers.[1] The jargon peculiar to Marxist writing (*hyena, hangman, cannibal, petty bourgeois, these gentry, lacquey, flunkey, mad dog, White Guard,* etc.) consists largely of words and phrases translated from Russian, German or French; but the normal way of coining a new word is to use a Latin or Greek root with the appropriate affix and, where necessary, the size formation. It is often easier to make up words of this kind (*deregionalize, impermissible, extramarital, nonfragmentary* and so forth) than to think up the English words that will cover one's meaning. The result, in general, is an increase in slovenliness and vagueness.

Meaningless words. In certain kinds of writing, particularly in art criticism and literary criticism, it is normal to come across long passages which are almost completely lacking in meaning.[2] Words like *romantic,*

[1] An interesting illustration of this is the way in which the English flower names which were in use till very recently are being ousted by Greek ones, *snapdragon* becoming *antirrhinum, forget-me-not* becoming *myosotis,* etc. It is hard to see any practical reason for this change of fashion: it is probably due to an instinctive turning-away from the more homely word and a vague feeling that the Greek word is scientific.

[2] Example: "Comfort's catholicity of perception and image, strangely Whitmanesque in range, almost the exact opposite in aesthetic compulsion, continues to evoke that trembling atmospheric accumulative hinting at a cruel, an inexorably serene timelessness. . . . Wrey Gardiner scores by aiming at simple bull's-eyes with precision. Only they are not so simple, and through this contented sadness runs more than the surface bittersweet of resignation." (Poetry Quarterly).

plastic, values, human, dead, sentimental, natural, vitality, as used in art criticism, are strictly meaningless, in the sense that they not only do not point to any discoverable object, but are hardly ever expected to do so by the reader. When one critic writes, "The outstanding feature of Mr. X's work is its living quality," while another writes, "The immediately striking thing about Mr. X's work is its peculiar deadness," the reader accepts this as a simple difference of opinion. If words like *black* and *white* were involved, instead of the jargon words *dead* and *living,* he would see at once that language was being used in an improper way. Many political words are similarly abused. The word *Fascism* has now no meaning except in so far as it signifies "something not desirable." The words *democracy, socialism, freedom, patriotic, realistic, justice,* have each of them several different meanings which cannot be reconciled with one another. In the case of a word like *democracy,* not only is there no agreed definition, but the attempt to make one is resisted from all sides. It is almost universally felt that when we call a country democratic we are praising it: consequently the defenders of every kind of régime claim that it is a democracy, and fear that they might have to stop using the word if it were tied down to any one meaning. Words of this kind are often used in a consciously dishonest way. That is, the person who uses them has his own private definition, but allows his hearer to think he means something quite different. Statements like *Marshal Pétain was a true patriot, The Soviet Press is the freest in the world, The Catholic Church is opposed to persecution,* are almost always made with intent to deceive. Other words used in variable meanings, in most cases more or less dishonestly, are: *class, totalitarian, science, progressive, reactionary, bourgeois, equality*.

Now that I have made this catalogue of swindles and perversions, let me give another example of the kind of writing that they lead to. This time it must of its nature be an imaginary one. I am going to translate a passage of good English into modern English of the worst sort. Here is a well-known verse from *Ecclesiastes*:

"I returned and saw under the sun, that the race is not to the swift, nor the battle to the strong, neither yet bread to the wise, nor yet riches to men of understanding, not yet favour to men of skill; but time and chance happeneth to them all."

Here it is in modern English:

"Objective consideration of contemporary phenomena compels the conclusion that success or failure in competitive activities exhibits no tendency to be commensurate with innate capacity, but that a considerable element of the unpredictable must invariably be taken into account."

This is a parody, but not a very gross one. Exhibit (3), above, for instance, contains several patches of the same kind of English. It will be seen that I have not made a full translation. The beginning and ending of the sentence follow the original meaning fairly closely, but in the middle the concrete illustrations— race, battle, bread—dissolve into the vague phrases "success or failure in competitive activities." This had to be so, because no modern writer of the kind I am discussing—no one capable of using phrases like "objective consideration of contemporary phenomena"— would ever tabulate his thoughts in that precise and detailed way. The whole tendency of modern prose is away from concreteness. Now analyze these two sentences a little more closely. The first contains forty-nine words but only sixty syllables, and all its words are those of everyday life. The second contains thirty-eight words of ninety syllables: eighteen of its words are from Latin roots, and one from Greek. The first sentence contains six vivid images, and only one phrase ("time and chance") that could be called vague. The second contains not a single fresh, arresting phrase, and in spite of its ninety syllables it gives only a shortened version of the meaning contained in the first. Yet without a doubt it is the second kind of sentence that is gaining ground in modern English. I do not want to exaggerate. This kind of writing is not yet universal, and outcrops of simplicity will occur here and there in the worst-written page. Still, if you or I were told to write a few lines on the uncertainty of human fortunes, we should probably come much nearer to my imaginary sentence than to the one from *Ecclesiastes*.

As I have tried to show, modern writing at its worst does not consist in picking out words for the sake of their meaning and inventing images in order to make the meaning clearer. It consists in gumming together long strips of words which have already been set in order by someone else, and making the results presentable by sheer humbug. The attraction of this way of writing is that it is easy. It is easier—even quicker, once you have the habit—to say *In my opinion it is not an unjustifiable assumption that* than to say *I think*. If you use ready-made phrases, you not only don't have to hunt about for words: you also don't have to bother with the rhythms of your sentences, since these phrases are generally so arranged as to be more or less euphonious. When you are composing in a hurry—when you are dictating to a stenographer, for instance, or making a public speech—it is natural to fall into a pretentious, Latinized style. Tags like *a consideration which we should do well to bear in mind* or *a conclusion to which all of us would readily assent* will save many a sentence from coming down with a bump. By using stale metaphors, similes and idioms, you save much mental effort, at the cost of leaving your meaning vague, not only for your reader but for yourself. This is the significance of mixed metaphors. The sole aim of a metaphor is to call up a visual image. When these images clash—as in *The Fascist octopus has sung its swan song, the jackboot is thrown into the melting pot*—it can be taken as certain that the writer is not seeing a mental image of the objects he is naming; in other words he is not really thinking. . . .

But if thought corrupts language, language can also corrupt thought. A bad usage can spread by tradition and imitation, even among people who should and do know better. The debased language that I have been discussing is in some ways very convenient. Phrases like *a not unjustifiable assumption, leaves much to be desired, would serve no good purpose, a consideration which we should do well to bear in mind,* are a continuous temptation, a packet of aspirins always at one's elbow. Look back through this essay, and for certain you will find that I have again and again committed the very faults I am protesting against. By this morning's post I have received a pamphlet dealing with conditions in Germany. The author tells me that he "felt impelled" to write it. I open it at random, and here is almost the first sentence that I see: "[The Allies] have an opportunity not only of achieving a radical transformation of Germany's social and political structure in such a way as to avoid a nationalistic reaction in Germany itself, but at the same time of laying the foundations of a co-operative and unified Europe." You see, he "feels impelled" to write—feels, presumably, that he has something new to say—and yet his words, like cavalry horses answering the bugle, group themselves automatically into the familiar dreary pattern. This invasion of one's mind by ready-made phrases (*lay the foundations, achieve a radical transformation*) can only be prevented if one is constantly on guard against them, and every such phrase anæsthetizes a portion of one's brain.

I said earlier that the decadence of our language is probably curable. Those who deny this would argue, if they produced an argument at all, that language merely reflects existing social conditions, and that we cannot influence its development by any direct tinkering with words and constructions. So far as the general tone or spirit of a language goes, this may be true, but it is not true in detail. Silly words and expressions have often disappeared, not through any evolutionary process but owing to the conscious action of a minority. Two recent examples were *explore every avenue* and *leave no stone unturned*, which were killed by the jeers of a few journalists. There is a long list of fly-blown metaphors would could similarly be got rid of if enough people would interest themselves in the job; and it should also be possible to laugh the *not un-* formation out of existence,[3] to reduce the amount of

---

[3] One can cure oneself of the *not un-* formation by memorizing this sentence: A *not unblack dog was chasing a not unsmall rabbit across a not ungreen field.*

Latin and Greek in the average sentence, to drive out foreign phrases and strayed scientific words, and in general, to make pretentiousness unfashionable. But all these are minor points. The defence of the English language implies more than this, and perhaps it is best to start by saying what it does *not* imply.

To begin with it has nothing to do with archaism, with the salvaging of obsolete words and turns of speech, or with the setting up of a "standard English" which must never be departed from. On the contrary, it is especially concerned with the scrapping of every word or idiom which has outworn its usefulness. It has nothing to do with correct grammar and syntax, which are of no clear importance so long as one makes one's meaning clear, or with the avoidance of Americanisms, or with having what is called a "good prose style." On the other hand it is not concerned with fake simplicity and the attempt to make written English colloquial. Nor does it even imply in every case preferring the Saxon word to the Latin one, though it does imply using the fewest and shortest words that will cover one's meaning. What is above all needed is to let the meaning choose the word, and not the other way about. In prose, the worst thing one can do with words is to surrender to them. When you think of a concrete object, you think wordlessly, and then, if you want to describe the thing you have been visualizing you probably hunt about till you find the exact words that seem to fit it. When you think of something abstract you are more inclined to use words from the start, and unless you make a conscious effort to prevent it, the existing dialect will come rushing in and do the job for you, at the expense of blurring or even changing your meaning. Probably it is better to put off using words as long as possible and get one's meaning as clear as one can through pictures or sensations. Afterwards one can choose—not simply *accept*—the phrases that will best cover the meaning, and then switch round and decide what impression one's words are likely to make on another person. This last effort of the mind cuts out all stale or mixed images, all pre-fabricated phrases, needless repetitions, and humbug and vagueness generally. But one can often be in doubt about the effect of a word or a phrase, and one needs rules that one can rely on when instinct fails. I think the following rules will cover most cases:

  (i) Never use a metaphor, simile or other figure of speech which you are used to seeing in print.
 (ii) Never use a long word where a short one will do.
(iii) If it is possible to cut a word out, always cut it out.
 (iv) Never use the passive where you can use the active.
  (v) Never use a foreign phrase, a scientific word or a jargon word if you can think of an everyday English equivalent.
 (vi) Break any of these rules sooner than say anything outright barbarous.

These rules sound elementary, and so they are, but they demand a deep change of attitude in anyone who has grown used to writing in the style now fashionable. One could keep all of them and still write bad English, but one could not write the kind of stuff that I quoted in those five specimens at the beginning of this article. . . .

In a more limited field American businessmen share Orwell's disgust with language which does not communicate. They pepper "subordinates with 'For-God's-sake-won't-you-people-learn-to-use-English-around-here' memos." *Fortune Magazine* **analyzes in detail the characteristics of the pompous jargon of American businesese: (1) Its vocabulary is uniform. (2) It relies on the passive voice. (3) It is wordy. (4) It borrows from the jargon of the government employee and of the social scientist. (5) It is dependent on euphemism. The theorem which** *Fortune* **formulates is of particular significance: "The less established the status of a person, the more his dependence on jargon."**

The Language of Business*

Not so long ago, the businessman used to take his language pretty much for granted. He could afford to. His place was respected and his authority unquestioned. And so he bought, he sold, he collected his bills, made an occasional speech perhaps—and if the public, the workers, or the government didn't quite understand what he was up to, well, so much the better for all concerned.

But no longer. Acknowledging the fact—and the necessity—of others' scrutiny, he has made the interchange of facts and ideas with them one of his principal jobs. The house organ, the interoffice memo, the press release, the press conference, the annual report —the range of his efforts has grown enormous. So widespread, indeed, that business has become almost as extensive a publisher as the government itself.

Is the language of business up to the job? The news

* Reprinted by special permission from the November, 1950, issue of *Fortune* Magazine; © 1950 by Time Inc.

—and refreshing news it is—is that the American businessman himself has begun to conclude that it is not. Some, in fact, have gone so far as to assert that the pomposity of management prose is the "root ill of our communication troubles." While that may be an overexcited judgment, management's surveys have demonstrated that a large amount of its language has been not only incomprehensible to the people it is trying to reach, but enormously expensive in money, time, and misunderstanding as well. "It is high time the American businessman discovered the English language—it would be very useful to him" . . . "We've turned our offices into paper mills" . . . "We love curt clear correspondence—but damned few of us know how to write it." Everywhere the chorus of self-criticism is growing.

The positive results of this self-examination have been impressive. In company after company, executives have been setting up "writing clinics" to scour management copy, staging correspondence-improvement courses, holding school in conference and public speaking techniques, and, at the very least, peppering subordinates with "For-God's-sake-won't-you-people-learn-to-use-English-around-here" memos. All of which is clearly to the good. At the same time— and not so clearly to the good—a school of experts has come forward to help the businessman by redesigning the language of industry. To accomplish this, the experts have developed a scientific method that, as we shall see later, has some disturbing implications. Meanwhile, a look at the anatomy of this language that is to be redesigned.

First, the written variety—and that infamous jargon, which, for want of a better term, we'll call businesese. Its signal characteristic, as the reader and all other critics of businesese will recognize, is its uniformity. Almost invariably, businesese is marked by the heavy use of the passive construction. Nobody ever *does* anything. Things *happen*—and the author of the action is only barely implied. Thus, one does not refer to something, reference is made to; similarly, while prices may rise, nobody *raises* them. To be sure, in businesese there is not quite the same anonymity as is found in federal prose, for "I" and "we" do appear often. Except when the news to be relayed is good, however, there is no mistaking that the "I" and "we" are merely a convenient fiction and that the real author isn't a person at all but that great mystic force known as the corporation.

Except for a few special expressions, its vocabulary is everywhere quite the same. Midwesterners are likely to dispute the latter point, but a reading of approximately 500,000 words of business prose indicates no striking differences—in the Midwest or anywhere else. Moreover, in sounding out a hundred executives on the subject, *Fortune* found that their views coincided remarkably, particularly so in the matter of pet peeves (principally: "please be advised," "in reference to yours of . . . ," "we wish to draw attention," "to acknowledge your letter"). The phrases of businesese are everywhere so uniform, in fact, that stenographers have a full set of shorthand symbols for them.

Because of this uniformity, defenders of businesese can argue that it doesn't make for misunderstanding. After all, everybody knows the symbols, and, furthermore, wouldn't a lot of people be offended by the terseness of more concise wording? There is something to this theory. Since businesese generally is twice as wordy as plain English, however, the theory is rather expensive to uphold. By the use of regular English the cost of the average letter—commonly estimated at 75 cents to $1—can be cut by about 20 cents. For a firm emitting a million letters a year, this could mean an annual saving of $200,000. Probably it would be even greater; for, by the calculations of correspondence specialist Richard Morris, roughly 15 per cent of the letters currently being written wouldn't be necessary at all if the preceding correspondence had been in regular English in the first place.

Where do the terms of businesese come from? Most, of course, are hand-me-downs from former generations of businessmen, but many are the fruit of cross-fertilization with other jargons. A businessman who castigates government bureaucrats, for example, is at the same time apt to be activating, expediting, implementing, effectuating, optimizing, minimizing, and maximizing—and at all levels and echelons within the framework of broad policy areas. Similarly, though he is amused by the long-hairs and the social scientists, he is beginning to speak knowingly of projective techniques, social dynamics, depth interviewing, and sometime soon, if he keeps up at this rate, he will probably appropriate that hallmark of the sound sociological paper, "insightful." Businesese, in fact, has very nearly become the great common meeting ground of the jargons.

Why do people who in private talk so pungently often write so pompously? There are many reasons: tradition, the demands of time, carelessness, the conservative influence of the secretary. Above all is the simple matter of status. Theorem: the less established the status of a person, the more his dependence on jargon.

Examine the man who has just graduated from pecking out his own letters to declaiming them to a secretary and you are likely to have a man hopelessly intoxicated with the rhythm of businesese. Conversely, if you come across a blunt yes or no in a letter, you don't need to glance further to grasp that the author feels pretty firm in his chair.

The application of euphemism, a favored device of businesese, further illustrates this status principle. Take the field of selling. At the top of the ladder you will find a great many people in it: *sales* managers, vice presidents for *sales*, etc. As you go down the ranks, however, it becomes difficult to find people in this line of work. Field underwriters, estate planners, merchandising apprentices, social engineers, distribution analysts, and representatives of one kind or another, yes. But *sales*men? Rarely.

Not only does businesese confer status, it protects it as well, by its magnificent usefulness for buck passing and hedging. "All you have to remember," one executive says, "is the one basis which characterizes all such intracommunication: let the language be ambiguous enough that if the text be successfully carried out, all credit may be claimed; but if the text be unsuccessfully carried out, a technical alibi can be set up out of the text itself."

For this purpose there is a regular subglossary of businesese. Most notable terms: "in the process of," "at this time," "under consideration," "in the not-too-distant future," "company policy," and, when one is unable to explain something properly, "obviously." People who have to submit periodic reports to their superiors are particularly dependent on such terms— salesmen, for example, would have a hard time if they couldn't report of some prospects that they were "very impressed." ("I am allergic to that word," says one sales manager. "It results in so few orders.")

The full application of businesese to hedging occurs when more than two heads are put to work on a problem. As the members of top management sit around the table, a relatively simple policy statement is introduced for discussion. This is kicked around a bit, as the saying goes, for though it certainly is a fine statement, couldn't agree with it more, there are just a few little angles and suggestions that maybe ought to be noted. Thereupon each executive, much as a baseball captain grasps a bat in choosing up sides, adds his qualification, until finally the original statement has been at once pointed up, toned down, given more dignity, made more forceful, altered to anticipate possible objections, concretized, amended, and resolved. Now no longer a mere statement but a philosophy, or collection of philosophies, it is turned over to the Public Relations Department to give to the waiting public. There is nothing, as so many people say, quite like what you get when everybody on the team works together.

Reverse Gobbledegook

Besides written businesese, there is another and far more influential category of business English. Generally, it is found in the spoken language of business— in particular, that brand to be heard at the banquet table, the convention, and the conference table.

It might best be called *reverse* gobbledegook, for in almost every outward respect it is the opposite of written jargon. Where written jargon is multisyllabic, the other is filled with short terse words; its sentences are short and their construction so much more active than passive that exclamation marks occur almost as frequently as periods. It is English that is on the beam, English with its feet on the ground; in short, *shirt-sleeve* English.

Thanks to reverse gobbledegook, the less you have to say, the more emphatically you can say it. All one has to do is use certain hard-hitting expressions, and refer as frequently as possible to the fact that these expressions are being used. A sure forewarning of its onrush, accordingly, is a prefatory announcement by the speaker that he is not going to beat around the bush, pull any punches, pussyfoot, use two-dollar words, or the like. The rest is inevitable; so standardized are the expressions of reverse gobbledegook that an audience would be stunned to attention were a single one of them altered by so much as a word. (One of these days a clever speaker is going to capitalize on this. "Gentlemen," he will say, "I offer a panacea.")

As a result, reverse gobbledegook can be self-defeating; that is, since its whole effect lies in the dynamic quality the words convey, their constant use tends to neutralize them. This can be overcome, however, by adding strengtheners—so that, in a very real sense of the word, it cannot be overemphasized that you sincerely, and unquestionably, meant what you said in the first place.

Like written businesese, reverse gobbledegook also confers status. For this purpose, it provides a sort of slang that, skillfully applied—particularly at the conference table—will impart to the user an appearance of savviness, cooniness, and general know-how. Want to mark yourself as a comer in the advertising field? Speak, then, of fun stories, sweet guys, the hard sell, straw men you set up to back into, and points you can hang your hat on. For each field you will find a sub-glossary, and, common to all of them, such universal terms as "play it by ear," "the pitch," "the deal," and the many expressions built on the suffix "wise." ("Budget-wise, Al, the pitch shapes up like this . . .")

Another characteristic of reverse gobbledegook is its dependence on analogy and metaphor. During a single banquet you may find business problems equated with an airplane, a broad highway, a boat being rocked, a river, a riverbank, a stream, a bridge, a train, a three-legged stool, and, sometimes, three or four of these things at once, in which case the passage is generally summed up with something like "It's as simple as that," or "That's all there is to the problem." (From a recent speech: "So business enterprise of America is trying to hone a sales force into the cutting-edge of an economy and there is a virus running rampant in the flock. Security-mindedness is a log across the stream when it comes to developing the optimistic salesman outlook.")

Outstanding is the great American football analogy. No figure of speech is a tenth as seductive to the businessman. Just why this should be so—baseball, curiously, is much less used—is generally explained by its adaptability to all sort of situations. Furthermore, the football analogy is *satisfying*. It is bounded by two goal lines and is thus finite. There is always a solution. And that is what makes it so often treacherous.

For analogy and metaphor can be insidiously attractive substitutes for thought. They are not, of course, when fleetingly used, when, as H. W. Fowler puts it (in *Modern English Usage*), they "flash out for the length of a line or so and are gone," but this is rarely the case in reverse gobbledegook. The user starts innocuously enough; his policy is *like* a thing-amajig in one respect. But only the stanchest mind can resist the analogy further. Before long he is entwined, and unconsciously operating on the premise that his policy *is* a thingamajig. The language, in short, has molded thinking, and the results can be a good bit more serious than a poor speech.

Besides written businesese, *Fortune Magazine* has told us, there is the spoken language of business, reverse gobbledegook, in which "the less you have to say, the more emphatically you can say it." To illustrate the characteristics of shirt-sleeve English, *Fortune* appends the following speech.

The Composite Business Speech*

This is not a parody. It is a loose compilation, based on a systematic count of the expressions and constructions most commonly used in current U.S. business speeches. Included are the sixty principal clichés of reverse gobbledegook.

Cooperation—An Opportunity and a Challenge
An Address

It is a pleasure and a privilege to be here with you today. These great annual meetings are always an inspiration to me, and doubly so today. After the glow-

* Reprinted by special permission from the November, 1950, issue of *Fortune* Magazine; © 1950 by Time Inc.

ing introduction by our toastmaster I must confess, however, that I'd like to turn the tables and tell a little story on Chuck. When I say it's about the nineteenth hole and a certain gentleman whose baritone was cracked, those of you who were at the Atlanta conference last year will know what I mean. But I won't tell it. Chuck Forbes is too good a friend of mine, and, seriously, I know full well we all realize what a tower of strength his yeoman service has been to the association in these trying times.

Yes, gentlemen, trying times. So you'll pardon me if I cast aside the glib reverberation of glittering generalities and the soothing syrup of sugar-coated platitudes and put it to you the only way I can: straight English.

We're losing the battle!

From every corner the people are being weaned from the doctrines of the Founding Fathers. They are being detoured from the high-speed highway of progress by the utopian highwaymen.

Now, the man in the street is a pretty savvy fellow. Don't sell him short. Joe Doakes may be fooled for a while, but in the end he wants no part of the mumbo jumbo the global saboteurs are trying to sell him. After all, he is an American.

But he has to be told.

And we're not telling him!

Now let me say that I do not wish to turn the clock back. None of us do. All forward-looking businessmen see themselves as partners in a team in which the worker is a full-fledged member. I regard our employees as our greatest business asset, and I am sure, mindful as I am of the towering potentials of purposeful energy in this group of clear-sighted leaders, that, in the final analysis, it is the rock foundation of your policies too.

But the team can't put the ball across for a first down just by wishing it. The guards and the tackles can't do their job if the quarterback doesn't let them in on the play. And we, the quarterbacks, are muffing the ball.

How are we to go over for a touchdown? My friends, this is the $64 question. I don't know the answers. I am just a plain-spoken businessman. I am not a soothsayer. I have no secret crystal ball. But I do know one thing: before we round the curve into the homestretch we have a job to do. It will not be easy. I offer no panaceas or nostrums. Instead, I would like to suggest that the real key to our problem lies in the application of the three E's.

What are the three E's?

ENTERPRISE! ENDEAVOR! EFFORT!

Each and every one of us must appoint himself a salesman—yes, a missionary, if you will—and get out and do some real grassroots selling. And when we hit the dirt, let's not forget the customers—the greatest asset any business has.

Now, much has been done already. But let's not fool ourselves: the surface, as our chairman has so wisely said, has hardly been scratched. The program is still in its infancy. So let me give it to you straight from the shoulder. The full implementation, gentlemen, depends on *us*.

So let's get on the beam! In cracker-barrel fashion, let's get down to earth. In good plain talk the man in the street can understand, let's remind Joe Doakes that the best helping hand he will ever find is the one at the end of his own shirt sleeve.

We have the know-how.
With sights set high, let's go over the top!

You will remember that Orwell commented that it should be "possible to laugh the *not un-* formation out of existence." Here Morris Bishop, Kappa Alpha Professor of Romance Literature at Cornell University and contributor of humorous verse to many magazines, does his best, while playfully sympathizing with the negative-lovers who run the risk of "one *not* too many."

MORRIS BISHOP

Not Unmindful of the Negative as I Am Not . . .*

"My sympathy with Mr. Schorer's general position is not inconsiderable."—*William M. Sale, in Epoch.*

Not inconsiderable is the sympathy I share
   With the negative-lovers, a not unplentiful lot,
Yet it is not impossible to be not unaware
   Of the disadvantages of the double and quadruple
      Not.

The negative fails of being not inexact;
   One Not too many, too few, and what have you got?
Your not innocuous Not will then react!
   If Not's not not, then prithee, what's Not not?

Ogden Nash, inventor of unusual rhymes, is the author of many collections of humorous verse, including *I'm a Stranger Here Myself* and *The Face Is Familiar.* Lightly satirical, Ogden Nash ridicules here the addict to the dull cliché and the vulgar euphemism.

* © 1949, The New Yorker Magazine, Inc.

Ogden Nash

Long Time No See, 'By Now*

Let us all point an accusing finger at Mr. Latour.

Mr. Latour is an illiterate boor.

He watches horse racing, instead of the sport of kings, when at the track,

And to him first base is simply first base, instead of the initial sack.

He eats alligator pear instead of avocado,

He says fan, or enthusiast, instead of aficionado.

He has none of the feeling for words that Ouïda and Spinoza felt,

Instead of Eleanor, he says Mrs. Roosevelt.

Sometimes he speaks even more bluntly and rashly,

And says the former Mrs. Douglas Fairbanks Senior, or the ex-Mrs. Clark Gable, instead of Sylvia, Lady Ashley.

He drinks his drinks in a saloon instead of a tavern or grill,

And pronounces Know-how, skill.

He calls poor people poor, instead of underprivileged,

Claiming that the English language is becoming over-driveleged.

He says the English language ought to get out of the nursery and leave the toys room,

So he goes to the bathroom instead of the little boys' room.

I will offer the hand of my daughter and half my income tax to him who will bring me the head of Mr. Latour on a saucer

* Reprinted by permission of the author. Originally published in *The New Yorker Magazine.* Copyright 1949 and 1951 by Ogden Nash.

Before he has everybody else talking as illiterate as
   Defoe and Chaucer.

   In "Politics and the English Language," George Orwell gave us this rule: "Never use a long word where a
short one will do." Now Frank Gelett Burgess (author
of "The Purple Cow" quatrain, *Goops and How to Be
Them,* and *Are You a Bromide?,* a satire on clichés)
has this to say: "If we use long words too much we are
apt to talk in ruts and use the same old, worn ways of
speech. This tends to make what we say dull, with no
force nor sting. But if we use short words we have to
say real things, things we know; and say them in a fresh
way. We find it hard to hint or dodge or hide or half say
things." (You will notice that the quoted passage contains only short words; no word has more than one
syllable. To prove his point, Burgess has written his essay entirely in short words.)

FRANK GELETT BURGESS

Short Words Are Words of Might*

This is a plea for the use of more short words in
our talk and in what we write. Through the lack of
them our speech is apt to grow stale and weak and,
it may be, hold more sham than true thought. For
long words at times tend to hide or blur what one
says.

What I mean is this: If we use long words too much
we are apt to talk in ruts and use the same old, worn
ways of speech. This tends to make what we say dull,
with no force nor sting. But if we use short words we
have to say real things, things we know; and say them

* Reprinted by permission of Louise Andrews. Copyright, 1939.

in a fresh way. We find it hard to hint or dodge or hide or half say things.

For short words are bold. They say just what they mean. They do not leave you in doubt. They are clear and sharp, like signs cut in a rock.

And so, if you would learn to use words with force and skill it is well first to use short words as much as you can. It will make your speech crisp and give zest and tang to what you say or write.

To prove that this is true, let us see what can be done here and now with short words. If I tell what I have to say in this plain way—that is, with naught but short words—you may think of it as but an odd freak of mine. But I hope it is more than a mere stunt. I shall try to show that one can say much that is true and live and with good strong meat of thought in it, in a way that does not come from books; that does not, as the phrase goes, "smell of the lamp."

Of course I need not be quite so strict and hold to a hard and fast rule. Some long words might be used and I could, I think, still prove my point. But I have thought that one might learn more and feel more sure that I am right from a talk which shows by its own form just what I would teach. And to do that I have made that form just as pure as it can be.

Well then, first, let us see just what place short words have in our tongue.

Short words must have been our first words when the world was young. The minds of men were raw, like that of a child. Their needs were few and so their thoughts were crude. Life for a man was in the main but a hunt for food, a fight with foes, a quest for a mate and a search for a place to rest safe from the storm and wild beasts. And for his mate there was thought but of their brat, the pot on the fire, the skins with which to make clothes.

Their first words were, no doubt, mere grunts or growls, barks, whines, squeals like those of the beasts. These rough, strange sounds were made to show how they felt. They meant joy or pain or doubt or rage, or fear—things like that. But these sounds came, in time, to grow more and more plain as real words. They were short words, strong and clear. And these first short words, used by our sires, way, way, back in the dark of time, still have strength and truth. They are bred in our flesh and bone. We may well call such words the life blood of our speech.

And so when we feel, we still use short words. If we know joy we say, "I love you more than all the world! Kiss me!" In our pride we cry, "I have got it! I have won!" With glee we shout, "Good for you! That is right!" And if we fear we use short words. We yell, "The house is on fire! Come quick!" We moan in our woe, "Oh, why have you done this!" or weep, "She is gone. She has left me!" We wail, "I am sick. I feel bad." All fierce moods, too, use short words. We snarl, "I hate you! You are a minx." We growl, "I will kill you!"

Most words we call bad are short words, too. A curse or an oath is bound to be made of short words. That is why such terms as damn and hell and worse words that stink of filth seem full of force to one who has the mind of a child—or a beast.

And words which to most seem still more vile, coarse sex words, they are short, as well. They must needs be since they tell of the stark, raw facts and acts of life. But at least they are not pale and weak. They do not slide off the truth. Nor do they gild dirt or mask low thoughts by sly tricks of speech as do some long words. What they mean they say right out and you know where you are with them.

Short words, you see, come from down deep in us —from our hearts or guts, not from the brain. For they deal for the most part with things that move and sway us, that make us act. And so they are said with not much heed of their use. We think out loud, that is all; and the words come to our lips as do smiles or scowls. At times we do not quite know how we use them—just as we do not know, much of the time, that we breathe; just as we walk, too, at times, with no care for our steps. That, I think, is why short words tend to make our thoughts more live and true. . . .

Long words have their use, of course. If you can say just what you mean in short words, those are the best words to use. But there are things that can not be said in short words. Then it is well to use long words, of course; but strive to use just as few as you can. Do not use a long or strange word when a short well-known word will do just as well. That is, if the main end you wish is to be clear.

Now, to use this rule, you should know that there are two kinds of long words. They came to be parts of our tongue each in its own way. One kind came in times of peace, and one, you might say, through war. Let us look at each kind in turn.

As men grew more wise, in the course of time they felt the urge to reach out to a world of pure thought and think of things they could not see or touch. These were vague things of the mind and soul, some as dim as dreams.

They would talk of such things to their friends; but more and more they found that they could not catch all these new thoughts, and hold them, so to speak, in a net of their old short words. The mesh was too coarse and thoughts got through it. They had to have words more fine.

And so they took short root words from old tongues. They would join two words to make one, change them a bit, put on heads or add ends to them to make them fit the mood and hue of their own speech. In this way the new words could not help but be long. Such new words were thus made a part of our tongue by a sort of slow growth.

Not a few long words, too, came in by way of the church. The priests and monks, of course, read, wrote and spoke the tongue of Rome. All the texts they used in the mass and church rites were of that tongue. The scribes used it in deeds and such scrolls, and the school men wrote their books in that old tongue. And so it is not strange that more and more those long words crept into the speech of folk who would show that they knew the ways of clerks and wise men. They came to be known in time to all, and each day it was less rare to find them in the mouths of plain men.

But we should take heed lest we grow too fond of these long words and let them lead us to care more for mere grace and rhythm than for good horse sense. For to some folk, though not all are such snobs, short words seem too blunt, too hard. They deem that the use of fine long words shows the rare mind of one who is not of the herd, a soul not kin to the fools and dolts who do not fear to say point blank that black is black and white is white.

This love of long words and pride in their use came to pass in one more way, though, and all at once, through war. I speak of the words that stem straight from the French tongue. The real cause which makes us like to use them, it may be, is that they are apt to bring to our minds the rich and great in the land, the high born, those who rule and look down on the rest. They are the smooth, slick words of ease and of the pomp and proud life of halls and courts.

In short, most of this kind of long words are the words of class, and short words are, for a large part, those of the mass, the plain folk. And this is why:

When the French duke with his men, in the days of yore, fought our sires and won our home land in the old world, just as he beat and put down the old earls and thanes and sent them off their lands and made the churls their slaves, so the French drove out the good old words of the soil and gave new names to most things.

It was like this: For one thing, the poor man might not kill the deer. That sport was now kept for the lord who held the land in fief. And so the serf, the rude swain, still knew the word deer, but it meant the live deer. There was a new word for the dead deer, the meat that the poor man might not eat, but was laid by the cook on the board of the lord for him and his men. Of course, since the lord was French, it was a French word. And so it was with all game, and for some time with the sheep and the hen and the ox, most of which were kept as food for the rich and great.

And so it was with a lot of things; the old words for the poor and the new French words for the rich. So it was with the names of the deeds the knights might do, but not the serf. The words that told of plain things, and toil, the poor folk kept. But those that had to do with the gay life of the court, the joust, the feast, words of sport or fray, were as bright and fine as the rich garb the high, vain French folk wore.

Nor was that all the change. A lot of words that show no trace of caste, verbs such as *to start, to stop, to end, to help, to go in, to go down, to woo, to win, to weep,* and a host of good old nouns, too, like *hap,* and *rede* and *weal* and *wrack* and *wight,* in time gave way to new French words. You might call these pairs twin words since they meant just the same thing. And the French words of these twins were held to be the more choice and to mark the well born.

In time, though, just as rich and poor mix in the town, so these two kinds of words came to mix. . . . And now we all use French words though some do not know that they are French. They are our own words now. Still, that is why, in the pride of birth or love of books (for the rude swain wrote no books), some like to speak or write with long words when they can—the words that flash and ring. It is thought that they give what they call style. Thus, more and more shun the short words of our bluff old sires, whose talk was plain talk and brisk and full of strength.

Though those old words, the short words, were tough and hale and in the speech of the poor did live on, most of them, a lot more died off or got lost and were known but by few, far in queer nooks.

So words like *clepe* (to call by name), *eke, fain, nill* (to will not to), *rathe* (near the dawn of day), *reave* (to spoil or rob), *swink* (a good old word that means to toil or drudge), *sooth* (true, real), *shend* (to blame or soil, or scorn), and *trow* and *ween* (to think it true), and a lot more of that stripe are known now but by bards and book men who use the speech of eld but as a sort of quaint game to show off their lore.

But why not try to bring some of those old words, that now seem so queer and strange to us, back to life in our talk? They are tart and have a fresh tang. They would be stout and true, to help to make our speech drive home what we mean. They would be as sharp as slang that has pep and pash that darts and gleams with the spry flash of wit. Speech with too few short words is like meat with no salt. . . .

Short words are words of might.

Dwight Macdonald, author of *The Ford Foundation: The Men and the Millions—An Unauthorized Biography,* contributes book reviews and "Profiles" to *The New Yorker.* Reviewing the Revised Standard Version of the Bible (R.S.V.), Macdonald, after careful examination of parallel passages in the King James Version (K.J.V.), finds the modern expository style of the R.S.V. ". . . direct and clear, and also flat, insipid, and mediocre." He concludes that "The exalted has become flat, the pungent bland, the rhythm crippled, phrases dear for centuries to English-speaking people have disappeared or are maimed."

When Orwell, in "Politics and the English Language," paraphrases a passage from Ecclesiastes, he demonstrates what happens when weak, vague abstractions are substituted for graphic, concrete illustrations. In "Short Words Are Words of Might" Burgess says, "But there are things that can not be said in short words."

In brief, with Macdonald's review, we turn from the general problem of meaningfulness as conceived by the other authors included in this section to a different

kind of communication—to poetic meaningfulness,
which speaks more through the connotation of words
than through their denotation; which speaks through
symbols, whose overtones circle out in widening waves
of meaning, and through rhythm, whose musical ac-
companiment reinforces meaning, expressing meaning
through sound.

Orwell, of course, states explicitly that he is concerned with accuracy and clarity, not with the *literary*
use of language. Admittedly, the problem of poetic language is too large for us to examine in this book; however, some sketchy indication of this rich aspect of
language is essential, for knowledge of language can increase aesthetic enjoyment of poetry and of style in
general. You will find a thoughtful introduction to this
subject in Margaret Schlauch's chapter "Language and
Poetic Creation" in her book *The Gift of Tongues*.

DWIGHT MACDONALD

The Bible in Modern Undress*

. . . If the Revisers had changed K.J.V. only where
modern scholarship found its translation defective, one
would hardly notice the alterations. But what they
are really translating is not the original Greek and
Hebrew but the English of the King James Version,
and the language they have put it into is modern expository prose, direct and clear, and also flat, insipid,
and mediocre. To accomplish this alchemy in reverse,
they have had to do a number of things. They have,
first of all, modernized the usage. "Thou," "ye," "thy,"
and "thine" are replaced by "you" and "your;" the
obsolete verb endings "-est" and "-eth" are dropped;
inverted word order is generally avoided; "unto" be-

* © 1953 The New Yorker Magazine, Inc.

comes "to," "whither" "where," "whatsoever" "whatever," and so on. This was done not for comprehen-
sibility, since any literate person knows what the old
forms mean, but as part of the policy of making the
Bible more "accessible" to the modern reader or listener. And, indeed, R.S.V. does slip more smoothly
into the modern ear, but it also slides out more easily;
the very strangeness and antique ceremony of the
old forms make them linger in the mind. The 1901
American Standard Version kept the old usage, and I
think rightly. For there are other considerations, too.
One is the loss of familiarity. It is extraordinary what
a difference modernization makes; even passages otherwise undisturbed have a blurred, slightly off-register
effect. The Hebrew Old Testament is an archaic docu-
ment, far more primitive even than Homer, and the
old usage seems more appropriate. "Thus saith the
Lord" is more Lordly than "Thus says the Lord,"
"Praise ye the Lord!" is more exalted than "Praise the
Lord!" The Ten Commandments lose when the awe-
some "Thou shalt not" is stepped down to the queru-
lous "You shall not;" the prophet Nathan's terrible
denunciation to King David, "Thou art the man!," col-
lapses in the police-report "You are the man!," and
God's solemn words to Adam, "Dust thou art, and
unto dust shalt thou return," are flattened in the conversational "You are dust, and to dust you shall return." A better case can be made for modernizing
the New Testament's usage, since it was written in
the everyday Greek of the common people. But the
Common Man of the first century A.D. was a considerably more poetic and (if he was a Christian)
devout creature than his similar of the twentieth century, and the religious passion of Jesus and Paul, tran-

scending modern experience, needs an exalted idiom
to be adequately conveyed. "Verily, verily I say unto
you" gets it better than "Truly, truly I say to you;"
Jesus's "Suffer the little children to come unto me"
(Mark 10:14) is more moving than R.S.V.'s "Let the
children come to me," which sounds like a mother at
a picnic.

The Revisers state that the old usage has been preserved in "language addressed to God or in exalted
poetic apostrophe." The first exemption has been respected—why God's own language should not also be
permitted some antique elevation I cannot see—but
the second often has not. Surely the Psalms are "exalted poetic apostrophe," yet in the Nineteenth Psalm,
"Day unto day uttereth speech, and night unto night
showeth knowledge" is diminished to "Day to day
pours forth speech, and night to night declares knowledge." Even the sacred (one would think) Twenty-
third Psalm comes out a bit fuzzy: "He makes me
lie down," for the rhythmic "He maketh me to lie
down," and instead of the triumphant "Yea, though
I walk through the valley of the shadow of death"
the tamer "Even though I walk." The most damaging effect of modernizing the usage is the alteration
of rhythm, which is all-important in a book so often
read aloud; quite aside from literary grace, the ceremonial effect of the Bible is enhanced by the interesting, varied, and suitable rhythms of K.J.V. But to
(partially) avoid inversion, the Revisers render "Male
and female created He them" (Genesis 1:27) "Male
and female He created them," breaking the rhythm's
back simply by changing the position of two words.
In K.J.V., Ecclesiastes moves to a slow, mourning
music;

What profit hath a man of all his labor which he taketh under the sun? One generation passeth and another generation cometh, but the earth abideth forever. . . . For there is no remembrance of the wise man more than of the fool for ever, seeing that which now is in the days to come shall all be forgotten. And how dieth the wise man? As the fool.

This now steps along to a brisker, less complex, and also less authoritative measure:

What does a man gain by all the toil at which he toils under the sun? A generation goes and a generation comes, but the earth remains forever. . . . For of the wise man as of the fool there is no enduring remembrance, seeing that in the days to come all will have been long forgotten. How the wise man dies just like the fool!

Ruth's familiar and moving "Whither thou goest, I will go" loses its cadenced charm when it is transmuted into "Where you go, I will go." So too, Philippians 4:8 ("Finally, brethren, whatsoever things are true, whatsoever things are honest, whatsoever things are just") is robbed of its earnest gravity when it is speeded up by replacing "whatsoever" with "whatever," just as Matthew 11:28 ("Come unto me, all ye that labor and are heavy laden") becomes inappropriately brisk when it is modernized to" Come to me, all who labor." I won't comment on changing Luke 16:3 from "I cannot dig; to beg I am ashamed" to "I am not strong enough to dig, and I am ashamed to beg.". . .

Other doubts swarm. I can't understand why "The spirit of God moved upon the face of the waters" had to be changed to "was moving over the face of the waters" or why the Nineteenth Psalm had to be altered from "The heavens declare the glory of God" to "The heavens are telling the glory of God." I don't

know why "there shall be weeping and gnashing of
teeth" (Matthew 22:13) had to become "there men
will weep and gnash their teeth" or why Paul's magnificent eloquence (in K.J.V., at least) has to be ham-
strung by pettifogging and needless alterations. For
example, in I Corinthians 13:1, "Though I speak with
the tongues of men and angels, and have not charity,
I am become as sounding brass or a tinkling cymbal"
is mutilated to "a noisy gong or a clanging cymbal,"
and in Ephesians 6:12, the familiar grandeur of "For
we wrestle not against flesh and blood but against
principalities, against powers, against the rulers of the
darkness of this world, against spiritual wickedness in
high places" is revised to "For we are not contending
against flesh and blood but against the principalities,
against the powers, against the world rulers of this
present darkness, against the spiritual hosts of wickedness in the heavenly places." Substituting "noisy
gong" for "sounding brass" and the weak, abstract
"contending" for the vivid "wrestle" seems to me ma-
licious mischief, if not assault and battery. . . .

The *raison d'être* of R.S.V., however, is not scholarly but stylistic; to produce a more "readable" Bible.
This being an age much more matter-of-fact than the
seventeenth century—or the first century for that matter—an age more used to skimming rapidly over a large
quantity of journalistic prose than to dwelling inten-
sively on a few poetic works, to make the Bible "readable" means to have it "make sense" to a reader who
wants to know simply What's It All About. Poetic
intensity or prophetic exaltation interferes with this
easy, rapid assimilation partly because such language
is idiosyncratic and partly because it strikes down to
depths of response which it takes time and effort for

the reader to reach. Literature, and especially religious literature, is not primarily concerned with being clear and reasonable; it is connotative rather than direct, suggestive rather than explicit, decorative and incantatory rather than functional. To make the Bible readable in the modern sense means to flatten out, tone down, and convert into tepid expository prose what in K.J.V. is wild, full of awe, poetic, and passionate. It means stepping down the voltage of K.J.V. so it won't blow any fuses. The Revisers have admirably and horribly succeeded; babes and sucklings (or infants) can play with R.S.V. without the slightest danger of electrocution.

In K.J.V., God describes the battle horse to Job: "Hast thou given the horse strength? Hast thou clothed his neck with thunder? . . . The glory of his nostrils is terrible. . . . He saith among the trumpets, Ha, Ha." R.S.V. steps it down to "Do you give the horse his might? Do you clothe his neck with strength? . . . His Majestic snorting is terrible. . . . When the trumpet sounds, he says, 'Aha!' " The trick is turned by replacing the metaphorical "thunder" with the literal "strength," by converting the thrilling "glory of his nostrils" into the prosaic "majestic snorting" (a snort can be many things, but never majestic), and toning down the wild "Ha, Ha" into the conversational "Aha!" A like fate has overtaken the Sermon on the Mount. Comparing this as rendered in K.J.V. and in R.S.V. is like hearing a poet read his verses while someone stands by and paraphrases. The exalted has become flat, the pungent bland, the rhythm crippled, phrases dear for centuries to English-speaking people have disappeared or are maimed. . . .

A Larger View

Language is more than a dictionary full of neatly classified, well-tamed words. Language is man's attempt to work out a "true-to-fact" understanding of his world; it is a system of gestures; it is magic, with a powerful, perhaps dangerous, life of its own. We speak of gaining power over words; according to many linguists, it is words which have power over us, for it is the very structure of our language which determines whether or not we shall be able to conceive certain ideas.

In the following section we shall hear these various concepts of language discussed by the semanticists and linguists. We shall read, too, of the movement to develop one world language for all men.

Anatol Rapoport, formerly assistant professor of mathematical biology at the University of Chicago, is at present with the Mental Health Research Institute, University of Michigan. Author of *Science and the Goals of Man* and of *Operational Philosophy,* he is also a regular contributor to S. I. Hayakawa's *Etc.: A Review of General Semantics.*

In the following article Rapoport undertakes to answer for the ordinary reader such questions as these: What is semantics? What is the difference between "ordinary semantics" and general semantics? What contributions has Alfred Korzybski made in the field of general semantics? Here Rapoport explains what symbolical logic is in its simplest terms and what the weaknesses of Aristotelian logic are that have necessitated the development of a system of non-Aristotelian logic.

Grammar, Rapoport says, "deals only with word-to-word relations." Logic is interested only in the relationship between assertions. ("If this is true, then that is true.") The semanticist goes farther. He is interested in *truth,* not merely in internal consistency. Assertions must be related to the world of fact. The general semanticist goes farthest. "He deals not only with words, assertions, and their referents in nature but also with their effects on human behavior." People do confuse words with things. They do "react to words as if they were facts," and as a result they are victimized by medicine men and demagogues. "Such reactions . . . make for persistent hostilities between groups; they make wars inevitable." Korzybski believes, Rapoport tells us, that through the principles of general semantics people can be trained to be saner in their linguistic habits and thus saner in their actions.

ANATOL RAPOPORT

What Is Semantics?*

. . . An embryologist may do a lot of things, but looking at embryos seems a significant part of his activity, just as one would expect. By analogy, many conclude that semanticists look at or for meanings;

* Reprinted from "What Is Semantics?" by Anatol Rapoport in *Language, Meaning and Maturity, Selections from ETC.: A Review of General Semantics, 1943–1953,* edited by S. I. Hayakawa, by permission of S. I. Hayakawa. Copyright 1954 by S. I. Hayakawa. "What Is Semantics?" Copyright 1952 by *American Scientist.*

so perhaps they have to do with dictionaries. This is not so. Dictionaries are the business of lexicographers. What, then, do semanticists do?

Who Are the Semanticists?

To answer this question, let us go to the writings of those who make frequent references to semantics or to equivalent terms which have to do with the study of meaning. We find that a number of prominent thinkers have occupied themselves with this study. In England these include Whitehead, Russell, Ogden, Richards, Ayer, and others; in Austria (later scattered, fleeing from fascism), a group of writers who called themselves the Vienna Circle, which included Carnap and Frank (now in the United States), Wittgenstein (now in England), and Neurath (deceased); the United States is represented by Charles Morris, and Poland by Korzybski (deceased) and Tarski, both of whom emigrated to the United States.

The next thing to be noted is that most of these writers have confined themselves to traditional academic work; they are for the most part professors of philosophy. But Korzybski's career was an exception. By training he was an engineer; he served as an officer in the Russian army and later as a League of Nations official. He never joined a university faculty. Rather, an educational institution of a special kind was built around him. What is most remarkable is that Korzybski's work has had *direct* impact, at least in this country, on a far wider range of people than the work of the philosopher-semanticists. For one thing, it captured the fancy of a number of keen, active men who saw the practical educational implications of semantics. One of them was Stuart Chase, who had been close to Roosevelt's "brain trust"; another was S. I. Hayakawa, a student of linguistics and professor of English. Others include Irving J. Lee, whose work was in speech; Wendell Johnson, psychologist and speech specialist; Francis P. Chisholm, another professor of English. All these men were deeply interested in how people use words and how words affect those who use them. They were able to translate some of the implications of Korzybski's work (properly referred to as *general* semantics) into the language of the college freshman, the perplexed citizen, and the teacher or mother who took her work seriously.

Two of the books written by them became booming best sellers (Chase's *Tyranny of Words* and Hayakawa's *Language in Action*). Hayakawa's book, Lee's *Language Habits in Human Affairs*, and Johnson's *People in Quandaries* became standard college texts; courses in "general semantics" cropped up in colleges and universities, and even in high schools; an International Society for General Semantics has a growing membership; and the Institute of General Semantics, founded by Korzybski, has remained a going concern after his death. The Soviets have seen fit to "expose" semantics as a new low in bourgeois philosophy,[1] and there have appeared similar blasts from the "right."

In view of this widespread interest, the workers in the field owe the general public an explanation. In the writer's opinion, such an explanation has been provided in S. I. Hayakawa's article "Semantics, General Semantics, and Related Disciplines." There the

[1] See, for example, B. Bykhovski, "The Morass of Modern Bourgeois Philosophy," *ETC.* VI (Autumn, 1948), 1–15.

history of semantics is reviewed, and the particular contribution of Alfred Korzybski is evaluated in the perspective of that history. . . .

To recognize the fruitfulness of Korzybski's ideas, one must relate his work to that of the academic semanticists (over the protests of both the academic scientists and the Korzybski-ites), and one must attempt to explain it in terms other than those coined by Korzybski. This we shall attempt to do. Let us therefore first look at "ordinary" semantics and then pass to general semantics.

Basic Principles of Semantics

Perhaps the most important ideas in semantics (with which modern logic is intimately interlaced) are (1) the propositional function, (2) the operational definition, (3) predictive value as the criterion of truth, (4) the theory of types.

The first and last of these are largely the work of Bertrand Russell. The second and third have a long history. They emerged with the development of modern physics and are already recognizable in the work of Ernest Mach, the exponent of the "positivist" approach to physics. Rudolf Carnap (a philosopher-logician) and P. W. Bridgman (a physicist) have stated the principles of operational definition and the predictive criterion of truth in unambiguous terms.[2]

Like most great ideas, these four principles are relatively easy to grasp. One wonders how the great thinkers of past centuries missed them. But evidently it is the same with great ideas as with great inventions:

[2] See Carnap, *Philosophy and Logical Syntax* (London, 1935); Bridgman, *The Logic of Modern Physics* (New York, 1927).

they seem simple only after one has been shown how.

Let us take the propositional function first. Classical logic (whose founder was Aristotle) took it for granted that all judgments could be broken up into simple propositions, that is, statements in which something (a predicate) is asserted about something (a subject). Examples are *water is wet; grass is yellow; some Greeks are rich; no animal is rational*. It was also assumed that such propositions were either "true" or "false"; *water is wet* is a true proposition; *grass is yellow* a false one. Logic was a set of rules for deriving propositions from other propositions. If *some Greeks are rich* is a true proposition, and *no Spartan is rich* is another true proposition, then *some Greeks are not Spartans* must also be a true proposition.

From the days of Aristotle to the nineteenth century hardly any important innovations were made in logic. Logic was considered largely a closed system (like euclidean geometry) and was taught in Western universities in much the same way Aristotle had taught it about 350 B.C.

The notion of the propositional function, however, was an innovation. The central idea of that notion is that one can make an assertion which *grammatically* looks like a proposition (a predicate asserted about a subject) but which cannot be said to be either true or false. An example of such a function is the statement *x is green*. One cannot tell, without knowing what *x* stands for, whether the statement is true or false. If *x* is grass, it is true, but if *x* is milk, it is false. The idea of the propositional function is obviously rooted in mathematics where statements like

$x^2 - 5x + 6 = 0$ are commonplace. It is evident that this statement is true if x stands for 2 or 3, but is false otherwise.

The propositional function is important in the theoretical development of logic. Just as arithmetic became algebra with the introduction of symbols to stand for variables (unknown quantities), so classical logic became symbolic logic with the introduction of the propositional function and of symbols to stand for propositions. Rules were developed for operating on propositions (like the rules of algebra which operate on variables), and logic became a branch of mathematics (or, one might say, mathematics was shown to be a branch of logic). And just as mathematics found wide application in science and technology, so symbolic logic is beginning to bear fruit in the design of computing machines, for example, and some theories of the structure of the nervous system.

But the notion of propositional function has another consequence more pertinent for this discussion. It showed that practically all our judgments are made not in terms of propositions but in terms of propositional functions! Consider the statement *grass is yellow*, which looks like a proposition. If by "grass" is meant the stuff that grows in Vermont in May the statement is false, but if one means the similar thing in California in July, then it is true! But then again it is not true if by "yellow" one means the color of ripe pumpkins.

Potentially, then, the question "What do you mean?" is pertinent at all times even when the "simplest" things are talked about, because the truth of statements depends on the meaning one assigns to the terms involved. This brings us to the second notion of semantics, the operational definition.

Again we must go back to Aristotle, because he made the first rules about definitions. According to Aristotle, a definition does two things. It places the thing defined in a class and then it tells how the thing is to be distinguished from other members of its class.

"Man is a featherless biped" is an aristotelian definition. It places man in a class of two-legged animals (bipeds) and distinguishes him from other members of that class such as birds (by the qualification featherless). Aside from the fact that plucked chickens and kangaroos are also featherless bipeds (as Norbert Wiener remarks), such definitions have even more serious pitfalls. Anything can be formally defined whether it exists or not. Furthermore, the class and the distinguishing characteristics, in terms of which aristotelian definitions are made, may be no clearer than the thing defined. If the purpose of definition is to make meaning clear, then many aristotelian definitions fail to do so. If a *xyphia* is defined as a three-legged bird, and if there are no three-legged birds, then *xyphia* is just as meaningless after having been defined as before. If *worry* is defined as a species of anxiety accompanied by hypertension, the definition is useless unless "anxiety" and "hypertension" are closer to our experience than "worry."

In contrast to the aristotelian definition by "class" and "characteristic," semanticists recommended the operational definition, which is widely used in science. An operational definition tells *what to do* to experience the thing defined. Asked to define the coefficient of friction, a physicist says something like this: "If a block of some material is dragged horizontally over a surface, the force necessary to drag it will, within limits, be proportional to the weight of the block. Thus the ratio of the dragging force to the weight is a constant quantity. This quantity is the coefficient of friction between the two surfaces." The physicist defines the term by telling *how to proceed* and *what to observe*. The operational definition of a particular dish, for example, is a recipe.

From the operational definition to the operational meaning of truth is only a step. Carnap and others distinguish two kinds of truth. One is the formal kind, based only on logical consistency within itself or with certain propositions *assumed* to be true. Carnap prefers to call propositions which are true in this sense "valid." For example, *If all x are y, and all y are z, then all x are z* is a valid proposition, because of its internal consistency independently of what *x*, *y*, and *z* stand for. The propositions of euclidean geometry are valid with respect to the postulates and axioms chosen for that geometry. One may also choose other postulates with respect to which some propositions of euclidean geometry will not be valid. Validity, then, has nothing to do with observation or experience.

A true proposition, on the other hand, must be related to some kind of experience. No amount of formal proof is sufficient to establish that grass is green. The decisive criterion is looking and experiencing greenness. In a way, the criterion involves a prediction of an experience: "Look and you will see that it is green." This is not to say, however, that "seeing is believing" is always a sound criterion. No amount of "seeing" will establish the roundness of the earth or the inverse square law of gravitation.

The criteria for these "facts" are indirect. They consist of certain experiments, the results of which are *predictable* if the roundness of the earth or the law of gravity is assumed true. If we assume that the earth is round, we can predict that departing ships will seem to sink into the horizon, and that the shadow on the moon during an eclipse will have a round edge, and that one can circumnavigate the earth.

Now we come to the fourth idea in semantics, the theory of types. It was known in antiquity that formal logic can be driven into a blind alley by a number of paradoxes. A typical one is the following. Consider the statement within this square.

> Every
> statement
> in this
> square
> is
> false.

Suppose the statement is true. Then, since it is the only statement in the square, it must be false. On the other hand, suppose it is false. Then, there must be true statements in the square. But again it is the only one; so it must be true. The example is trivial, of course, but similar paradoxes arise in mathematics and make difficulties for mathematicians. Since progress in mathematics depends on its complete internal consistency, it was necessary to re-examine the logical foundations of mathematics. One of the results of this re-examination is the theory of types. The theory rests on the principle that "a class cannot be a member of itself." That is, if you make a statement about *all* statements of a certain class, the statement you have made cannot be itself considered to be in that class. This was the principle violated in the paradox just described.

Principles of Korzybski's General Semantics

Now let us look at Korzybski's basic principles (or the non-aristotelian postulates, as they are sometimes called), on which his "non-aristotelian system" is built: (1) the principle of non-identity, (2) the principle of non-allness, (3) the principle of self-reflexiveness.

As we shall see in a moment, logically the first principle is included in the second, so that it can be omitted. But we shall also see that, from the point of view of further development of Korzybski's system, there is a very good reason for not omitting it, and even for putting it first. However, we shall look first at the second principle. To use Korzybski's figure of speech, it says, "The map does not represent all of the territory"; that is, no matter how good a map you make, you cannot represent all of the territory in it. Translated in terms of language, it means that no matter how much you say about some "thing," "event," "quality," or what not, you cannot say *all* about it. The connection between this principle and the notion of propositional function is not hard to trace. According to the latter, *grass is green* is a propositional function, because both "grass" and "green" are variables. Grass can refer to vegetation in Vermont, Kentucky, or California. Green can range over the color of canaries, emeralds, or gall. Therefore, even such simple propositions as "grass is green," "the earth is round," etc., can be true only within limits.

Now let us go back to the first principle, which can be stated as "The map is not the territory"; that is, the word is not the thing it represents. Clearly, if the map does not even *represent* all of the territory, it cannot *be* the territory. So logically there is no need to state the principle of non-identity in addition to that of non-allness. However, the development of Korzybski's non-aristotelian postulates implies far more than relations between language and fact. His big point is that the structure of our language affects the *functioning of our nervous systems*, and this is where his work departs radically from that of the "classical" semanticists. To say "the word is not the thing it signifies" is not just to indicate the obvious. It is to draw attention to a fundamental inadequacy of human behavior and to trace this inadequacy to the interaction of nervous systems with language.

According to Korzybski (and his idea is corroborated by numerous psychological and psychiatric findings), people do behave *as if* they identified words with things. Identified does not mean "equated verbally." Practically everyone will agree that the *word* Negro is not the same as Mr. Smith, to whom the label Negro is applied. Nevertheless many people, in judging Mr. Smith, react to the label rather than to Mr. Smith. To take another example, a man may react to some situation, say a rejected application for a particular job, by labeling the situation "I am a failure." He may then react to the label in ways that are far removed from an effective remedy of the situation.

The orientation recommended by Korzybski to

free the individual from the tyranny of words was called by him *extensional*. Roughly speaking, to be extensional is to be aware of things, facts, and operations in the way they are related in nature instead of in the way they are talked about. The extensionally oriented person differentiates better than the word-minded (intensionally oriented) one. He is aware of the basic uniqueness of "things," "events," etc., and so he is more aware of *change* than the intensionally oriented person, who mistakes the fluid, dynamic world around him for the static, rigid world of labels, "qualities," and "categories" in his head.

The extensional orientation of Korzybski is quite analogous to the "operationalism" of semantics. An operational definition is essentially an extensional definition, because it tells what to *do* (instead of what to say) to bring the thing defined within the range of experience. Likewise the criterion of predictive value in establishing truth is basically extensional. According to this criterion, statements, assertions, judgments, principles—in short, all kinds of talking—are rated much as checks are rated in our economy: they are accepted if one is reasonably sure they can be backed by currency. For an extensionally minded person, words that cannot be defined by operations, and statements that do not by implication contain predictions of experience, are like checks on nonexistent accounts.

This brings us to the third non-aristotelian postulate of self-reflexiveness. An ideal map of a territory, says Korzybski, would have to include a map of itself, if the map were part of the territory. But then it would have to include the map of the map of itself, etc., without end. This principle is illustrated on some packages, on which there is a picture of the package itself, which in turn contains another picture of itself, etc. To avoid this difficulty, the principle of non-identity is extended to the more general principle of multiordinality. The map is not the territory. Neither is map_2 of the map_1 itself a map_1. A map of map_2 would then be a map of the third order, etc., etc. In terms of language, this means that theoretically we may have a $language_1$ about things, a $language_2$ about $language_1$, etc. As Korzybski himself points out, this principle is an outgrowth of Russell's theory of types. It has "counterparts" in classical semantics, where logicians talk about languages of different order (metalanguages). In terms of human behavior, this suggests that one may react to the world, then react to his reaction, then to reactions of higher order, etc.

Thus Korzybski's principles have a close relation to semantic principles. It follows that the whole Korzybskian system is an outgrowth of semantics. But the Korzybskian system goes much further. When its implications are worked out, it will be as far removed from semantics as semantics is from logic, and as logic is from grammar.

Grammar deals only with word-to-word relations. It teaches how to put words together into a sentence. It is not interested in how sentences are related to each other or how they are related to facts. Logic goes further. To a logician, sentences are assertions, and he is interested in relations between assertions (if this is true, then that is true). But for the logician words need not have any meaning except as defined by other words, and the assertions need not have any relation to the world of fact. The semanticist goes

further than the logician. To him words and assertions have meaning only if they are related operation-
ally to referents. The semanticist defines not only
validity (as the logician does) but also truth. The
general semanticist goes the furthest. He deals not
only with words, assertions, and their referents in nature but also with their effects on human behavior.
For a general semanticist, communication is not
merely words in proper order properly inflected (as
for the grammarian) or assertions in proper relation
to each other (as for the logician) or assertions in
proper relation to referents (as for the semanticist),
but all these together, with the chain of "fact to nervous system to language to nervous system to action."

General semantics may indeed be considered of
fundamental importance in the science of man. In
Gestalt psychology, phenomenological psychology,
psychiatry, and cultural anthropology, the "neurolin-
guistic" factors of human behavior are assuming an
ever greater importance. Human experience (according to the views developed in those disciplines) consists of *selecting* certain ones out of innumerable
stimuli in the environment; and human behavior consists of *organizing* experiences along certain patterns.
There is strong evidence that both the selecting and
the organizing patterns bear a definite relation to the
structure of language and to linguistic habits. . . .

"Exclamations of all sorts rise out of a compelling
impulse to *voice* emotion. . . . How make a word convey not only its dictionary meaning, but all of the
emotion which may be associated with it? A simple
answer is found in pitch and volume, expression and

gesture—a shrug of the shoulders, a wave of the hands."
With this introduction, Burges Johnson (who has taught
English at Vassar College and at Syracuse University,
has served on the staff of Harper & Brothers, and has
published many books of light verse) traces for us the
degeneration of the once terrible curses, with "vestiges
of magic" still clinging to them, as they have become
more familiar and have faded away into ordinary ex-
clamatory noises and finally into "mere habit of speech."

BURGES JOHNSON

The Oath Interjectional
(or Exclaiming)*

. . . Exclamations of all sorts rise out of a compelling
impulse to *voice* emotion. How to communicate ideas
is a fairly simple problem, calling first for a dictionary
and then for some skill in word arrangement. But how
express feeling? How make a word convey not only
its dictionary meaning, but all of the emotion which
may be associated with it?

A simple answer is found in pitch and volume,
facial expression and gesture—a shrug of the shoulders, a wave of the hands. These might be enough
without words. Or they may even contradict the words.
An idea worded in an ordinary tone may mean what
the dictionary says it does but shrieked it means something else. An old curse, uttered pleasantly, may mean
no more than a whimsical greeting, but in another
tone it is converted into an insult. "When you say
that, smile!"

Man expresses his strongest emotions by noises
which mean nothing at all in the dictionary. He cries,

* Copyright by Burges Johnson; reprinted by permission of the
author.

"Ouch!" or "Oi oi!" or "Ha ha!" or "Whoops!" or "Wirra wirra!" or he utters an unspellable groan or scream or sobbing sound, and anyone who hears him guesses the nature of his feeling and how much he feels it. His emotions demand a language of their own, and it is important for us to understand it. . . .

Man invented his first curse words to give form and force to his malign wishes; and he invented swearwords to back up vows and establish his veracity. As time passed, he forgot both the purpose and the meaning of most of these terms; but he still remembers the words themselves and feels that he gains emphasis by the use of them and an outlet for his emotions.

The curse of Holy Mother Church, which threatened social ostracism during the offender's lifetime and eternal torment after death, provided a mighty phrase. There was emphasis for you! But all the layman has left of "May you suffer eternal damnation!" is "damn"—now no more than a small protesting noise to suggest that there is a grain of sand in the spinach or that the fountain pen leaks. It is used so generally for mild emphasis in English that a Frenchman searching for its equivalent when translating an English novel hit upon *très* as the only French term of equal weight. . . .

Many of the early oaths, sonorous sentences long, shrank in size as they shrank in power, and now are single words surviving only in period novels. First asseverative, then denunciatory, they have ended up as meaningless ejaculations. "I swear by God's mercy" became "Gramercy!" "May God strike me blind!" became "Blimey!" "May God condemn me!" became "Damme!" "By my Faith!" shrank to "Faith," an interjection now obsolete except among the Irish, who use it to start any sentence, without even the dignity of an exclamation point. "I swear by our Lady," according to good authority, became "Bloody," and would have died out completely if the British had not imagined a new significance for it in its shrunken form and banned it from society. This renewed its life; it made a new loud noise so long as society frowned upon it. But now that it has passed the censors of the London stage and actually been spelled out in the columns of the *London Times*, it will soon lose the little value it has left, even among London cabbies and Billingsgate fishwives. . . .

Whenever men lose reverence for such names or fear of such laws, but know that people all about them still retain such an attitude, they find themselves with a rare equipment of noisy emphasis. Then finally, when the name itself has become slurred or misshapen and almost unrecognizable they continue to use it as a mere habit of speech; not so much sounding brass as a tinkling symbol.

Another phenomenon of human behavior would more greatly amuse a visitor from Mars. Men who longed to shout holy names at one another, for the effect they might have, feared a kickback. To hurl the name of Deity might make a foe tremble, but suppose the Deity took offense and did something about it? The everyday profanity of our Calvinist ancestors is worth studying.

Bootleg profanity (or Deaconic swearing) came into being when men attempted to use the names of God and His saints and His holy places in verbal attack, or merely for emphasis, and hoped God wouldn't know about it. Then were born "Gosh!" and "Gol!" and "For Land's sake!" and "Lordy!" "Laws-a-massy!" "Dad burn it!" "Dog blast it!" "Doggone it!" "By Golly!" "By Gum!" "Gee Rod!" "Dog blank it!" "Bless my stars!" "Blast it!" "Dod blast it!" "Blat it to smitherines!" "Gast!" "Dod gast it!" "Flabbergast!" "Blow!" "I'll be blowed!" "Confound it!" "Drat it!" "Goodness grieve us!" "I'll be jiggered!" "Dod rot it!" and a thousand ingenious variations. These of course included reference to the attributes of God without using his name: "Goodness," "Gracious," "Mercy," "Almighty" and the like. . . .

"Blast" and "blasted" are oddities. Their value lay in the fact that blasting of a human being was obviously an act of an angry God. So the word was at one time looked upon as profane, and little boys had their mouths washed out with soap if they used it. Now it is a rarity, having a mild intensifying value. . . .

Joseph Pulitzer, of the New York World, who is referred to by Mr. Mencken as a great master of profanity in three languages, is credited with the intensified term "Don't be so indegoddampendent." Certainly the phrase was common parlance on Park Row in my own reportorial days. Mr. Mencken adds the retort of managing editor Coates to that charge, "I'm under no obligoddamgation to do that and I won't."

The drawing-room ejaculations of the sixteenth century have come down to us in its literature; most of them, though they had once been solemn oaths, have long since shriveled up and died. "By the Masse!" "What the good yeare!" "Tille valle, tille valle!" appearing in *Henry IV* as "Tillyfally!" and defined by Webster as an obsolete equivalent of "Fudge!" "Marry!" which long before had been "By Mary!" had come to mean no more than "Indeed!" "By sweete Sanct Anne!" "By cocke!"

"By gog!" "By cocks precious potstick!" "Cocks-nownes!" "By the armes of Caleys!"—these and many others are found in the sixteenth-century play, "Roister Doister." Also such exclamations as: "Oh lorde, hoigh dagh!" "I dare sweare!" "I shall, so God me save!" "I make God a vow!" "A mischief take his token and him and thee too!"

In *Henry IV*, we find "What a devil!" "What a pox!" "By'r lady!" "Zounds!" " 'S blood!" "God's body!" "By the masse!" "A plague on thee!" "By cock and pie!" "I'm a Jew else!" "I'm a rogue if I do!"

In literature of the same period we find "Y faith!" "Bir Lord!" "Bir Lady!" "Ile be sworne!" "God's precious soles!" " 'S foot!" " 'Sbodie!" "God's my life!" "God's my passion!" " 'Sleight!" " 'Sdeath!"

The seventeenth century bequeaths to us the greatest variety of mild parlor swearing, and most of it has also been allowed to die. I am indebted to Mr. Henry Cecil Wyld for collecting these from the literature of the time, such as the plays of Otway, Congreve, Wycherley and others: "Let me die!" "Let me perish!" "Strike me speechless!" "Strike me down!" "Death and eternal tortures!" "Burn me if I do!" "Rat me!" "Never stir!" "I'll take my death!" "As I'm a person!" "Stap my vitals!" "Split my windpipe!" "As I hope to breathe!" "I'm a dog if I do!" "By the universe!" "I swear and declare!" "I do protest and vow!" "I protest I swoon at cere-

mony!" "I profess ingenuously!" "Gads my life!"
"O Crimine!" "O Jeminy!" "Gad take me!" "I'll
lay my life!" "By the Lord Harry!" "Gadzooks!"
"Gad's bud!" "Gud soons!" "Marry-gep!" " 'Sheart!"
"Eh Gud, eh Gud!" "Zoz!" "Ad's soz!" "D's dig-
gers, Sir!" "Od's heart!" "Adsheart!" "Gadswoons!"
"Marry come up, my dirty cousins!" "Lard!" "As
sure as a gun!" . . .

Gone are the echoing oaths of a day when swearing was at least an art. Then swashbuckling phrases
went with swashbuckling deeds. "Devil take thee,
Bastard, thou didst parry that one! But by the bones
of St. Michel, I swear this point will now spit thy
cringing gizzard!" . . .

Otto Jespersen (1860–1943), Danish philologist and
formerly professor at the University of Copenhagen, is
the author of *Language: Its Nature, Development and
Origin*, and of *Growth and Structure of the English
Language*.

Writing of the "name superstitions and word taboos"
of primitive societies scattered over the earth, Jespersen
expresses the linguist's point of view that "We shall
never thoroughly understand the nature of language,
if we take as our starting point the sober attitude of
the scientifically-trained man of today who regards the
words he uses as means for communicating, or maybe
further developing, thought. To children and savages a
word is something very different. To them, there is
something magical or mystical in a name. It is something that has power over things. . . ." By a study of
our own modern euphemisms for *die* and *death*, Mr.
Jespersen shows that it is not only the members of primitive societies who fear words. (We are reminded of

Rapoport's discussion of the problem that people often "react to words as if they were facts.")

Jespersen states, too, that "It is now coming to be generally recognized by linguistic investigators that such name taboos have great influence on the evolution of vocabulary." That is, tabooed words have been lost in certain languages as they have been replaced by acceptable circumlocutions. This observation will no doubt be important in future linguistic investigations.

OTTO JESPERSEN

Mysticism of Language*

. . . We shall never thoroughly understand the nature of language, if we take as our starting point the sober attitude of the scientifically-trained man of today, who regards the words he uses as means for communicating, or maybe further developing, thought. To children and savages a word is something very different. To them, there is something magical or mystical in a name. It is something that has power over things and is bound up with them in a far more intimate manner than we are wont to imagine. This view may begin very early in the child's life. The child that notices that it does not get anything if it does not ask for it nicely, but that its parents at once fulfill its wishes when it says 'water, please,' rejoices in the magical power he has come to possess by the utterance of these syllables. As Sully expresses it: 'children regard names as objective realities mysteriously bound up with the things, and, in a manner, necessary to them. A nameless

* Reprinted from *Mankind, Nation and Individual* by Otto Jespersen, by permission of George Allen & Unwin Ltd. Copyright 1946 by George Allen & Unwin Ltd.

object is, for a child, something incomplete—almost uncanny,'[1] and 'the childish tendency is to "reify" the name, that is, to regard it as part of the real thing itself, instead of something extraneous and arbitrarily attached to it.'[2]

We meet similar conceptions among the savage tribes of very different parts of the globe.[3] Knud Rasmussen several times describes the Greenlanders' view of the Name as something self-existent: 'They divide a person into a soul, a body, and a name. . . . The name is a soul, with which a certain stock of vital power and dexterity is bound up. A person who is named after a dead man, inherits his qualities, and the dead man is not at rest, his life's-soul cannot pass to the land of the dead, until a child has been named after him. Connected with this view is the fear of mentioning a dead man's name, before a child has received it, lest the man should thus lose some part of its virtue. After the death of the body, the name takes up its abode in a pregnant woman, and keeps her inwardly pure during her pregnancy; then it is born with the child.'[4]

Connected with such superstitious conceptions are the customs found under varying forms in many other parts of the world for perpetuating a man's name. Some of the facts were brought to light by Gustav Storm, who succeeded in drawing from them some interesting conclusions in regard to Scandinavian history in the Middle Ages. A collection of

[1] *Nineteenth Century*, November, 1891, p. 739.
[2] *The Human Mind*, 1892, p. 312.
[3] The magical power of the Name is treated psychologically in C. K. Ogden and I. A. Richards' *The Meaning of Meaning* (London, 1923).
[4] *Nye mennesker*, pp. 121, 130: *Grønland*, p. 124.

other material is to be found, *e.g.* in Feilberg's Jut-
land Dictionary under the word 'navn' [name],
where many references are given. The main principle
in old times was that a child was called after that
relative, recently dead, whose soul and power and
luck it was desired that the child should inherit, on
the supposition that these things would come to the
child with the name. Long after this conception had
passed, it lived on in customs connected with the
naming of children. So in many places there was a
disinclination to give a child its father's name, unless
the latter had died before the child's birth, in which
case the child took his name almost as a matter of
course. So, children were named much more frequently after dead grandparents than after living
ones. Many other peculiar points with regard to the
naming of children find a simple explanation, when
the ideas of a primitive race on the nature and vital
significance of the name are taken into account.

Many primitive peoples are afraid of mentioning
their name to strangers: it is a part of their being,
and they do not wish others to get power over them
by knowing their names (Niceforo GA. p. 208 f.).
The Sakalava's in Madagascar are not allowed to
communicate to strangers either their own name or
the name of their village, for fear the strangers should
make a mischievous use of it. (Walen).

In some Australian tribes everyone has two names:
—a general name, and a special name only known to
members of his totem-group (Spencer and Gillen).
The Araukans carefully conceal their personal-name
from strangers: in their presence they are called by
their family-name. Near Tyer's Lake in Victoria the
natives mention no one by his name, but call him

brother or cousin, or use designations like the left-handed one, the little fool (Lefébure).

In South Italy a man who is suspected of being a 'jettatore,' having the 'evil eye,' is never spoken of by name, but only as 'he who cannot be named' or 'Mr......, let us not name him.' It is thought that the mere naming of the 'jettatore' brings ill-luck, just as much as seeing or touching him. (Niceforo GA. 210.)

In popular belief as reflected in fairy-tales, songs, and traditional legends, we find again and again the idea that knowledge of the name of a person or thing gives one power over the person or thing. One example must suffice. When St. Lawrence was building the cathedral at Lund, he received supernatural assistance from a goblin ('trold') who by way of reward was to have the saint's two eyes unless the latter could name his name. When the church was nearly finished, Lawrence heard a woman on a little hill outside the town hush her weeping children with the promise that their father Finn was soon coming with gifts for them. Lawrence could therefore hurl the name at the goblin, who on the instant lost his power and was turned to stone.[5]

A similar magical power, according to popular belief, lies in various formulas, which, if spoken or merely written, are powerful enough to keep anything evil away, to cure sickness, bring good to him who knows them and applies them, and cause harm to his enemy. Such formulas are found in all coun-

[5] Connected with this is the great mystical importance assigned in various poems of the Edda (e.g., Vafþrúþnismál, and especially Alvismál) to knowledge of names, especially of the names of gods and things connected with the gods.

tries: they often contain words or fragments of words which are not intelligible. Here I will only bring evidence from Greenland where, according to Knud Rasmussen,[6] one finds charms with old untranslatable, apparently meaningless, words which old men have dreamt. 'They are handed on from generation to generation. Everyone regards them as of great value, but he is not allowed to impart them till he feels the approach of death.'

It is also well-known what great magical importance has been attached in many places to words or letters, scratched or written in different ways on different objects, to give the writer power over persons or things. The runes were originally not so much means of communications as charms. One of the most important passages for the understanding of the subject is the stanzas woven into the songs about Sigurd in the Edda, in which it is said:

> Winning-runes learn, if thou longest to win,
> And the runes on thy sword-hilt write;
> Some on the furrow, and some on the flat,
> And twice thou shall call on Tyr.

> Ale runes learn, that with lies the wife
> Of another betray not thy trust;
> On the horn thou shalt write, and the backs
> of thy hands,
> And Need (N) shall mark on thy nails.

> Birth-runes learn, if help thou wilt lend,
> The babe from the mother to bring.

And thus it goes on with sea-runes, medicinal runes, and runes of wisdom.

[6] *Grønland*, p. 123.

> Speech-runes learn, that none may seek
> To answer harm with hate. . . .
>
> Thought-runes learn, if all shall think
> Thou art keenest minded of men.[7]

. . . It is now coming to be generally recognized by linguistic investigators that such name-taboos have had a great influence on the evolution of vocabulary. So in many places the proper name for the 'bear' has been lost. In Lapland people are so much afraid of its killing the cattle that they do not call it by its usual name *guouzhja*, but say *moedda-aigja*, which means 'grandpapa with the skin coat' (Leem, Nyrop, p. 30): other names also are given. In Siberia the Yakuts call the bear Our lord, famous old man, good father, and so on. This helps us to understand how the old Aryan name for the bear, which we know from the Gk. *arktos*, Sk. *rkṣah*, Zend *aršo*, Lat. *ursus*, Erse *art*, etc., has entirely disappeared in a number of related languages, and has been replaced by different circumlocutions: Slavonic *medvědi*, Russian *medvěd*, which originally means 'honey-eater,' Lithuanian *lokys*, which probably means 'the sweet-toothed,' and the Danish *bjørn*, Germ. *bär*, Engl. *bear*, which means 'the brown.'

. . . Finally, we have the special 'women's language,' found in many different parts of the world. Often it merely includes a number of expressions specially used by women (or by women and children). But often it also embraces special grammatical forms or customary pronunciations; but all these peculiarities are largely or entirely dependent on old beliefs, according to which certain words and ex-

[7] *Sigrdrifomál* 6 ff., transl. by H. A. Bellows, New York, 1923.

pressions are taboo for certain persons and must therefore be replaced by other words, by noa-words.[8]

It has often been remarked how tenaciously savage races cling to everything that is traditional: how, for example, they fashion and employ their tools without deviating a hair's breadth from the manner in which their ancestors did before them. This conservatism has rightly been recognized[9] as resulting from an active faith in the things' possessing mystical properties, the potency of which depended on the objects' forms, so that by making the least change in them one would lose one's power over them. Mysterious dangers were threatened if anything was changed. For similar reasons primitive races cling with equal tenacity to their inherited language. Of course mutations of language to a great degree elude human observation, and it therefore happens that without the natives detecting it, their language does alter little by little with the daily use made of it and with its transmission to new generations. But, so far as they can, they see to it strictly that nothing shall be changed (apart from the case where a belief in the mystical power of the name actually demands the adoption of new words) and the most scrupulous watch is kept that there should be no change in the holy forms of religious worship and ceremonial hymns. It is owing to this careful watch over the old traditional sounds of words that the old Vedic hymns of the Indians have been orally preserved with such great fidelity that we are acquainted with their forms and pronunciation to the minutest detail. According to Sylvain Lévy, the old Vedic language was to such

[8] See my *Language*, Chap. XVI.
[9] See Lévy-Bruhl FM p. 35.

an extent an exclusively religious language, that it was not till the arrival of conquerors from without who were strange to Indian tradition that people dared to employ Sanskrit in profane literature.

While, then, in discussing the fear of mystical effects from the use of one word instead of another, we spoke, from our civilized standpoint, of *superstition*, here, where we are speaking of keeping unchanged what one's ancestors have handed down to one, we will rather regard this as an outcome of a commendable religious feeling, closely allied to the warm feeling with which each one of us conceives his own native language as a holy national inheritance.

In his novel *Nineteen Eighty-Four*, George Orwell, whose essay "Politics and the English Language" we have read earlier, tells a nightmare story of the totalitarian society of 1984 in which Big Brother finally ferrets out, persecutes, and wins over the last surviving rebel for individual freedom.

As an appendix, George Orwell includes the following essay on "The Principles of Newspeak," the language of Ingsoc, or English Socialism. Designed to diminish the range of thought, "the purpose of Newspeak was not only to provide a medium of expression for the world-view and mental habits proper to the devotees of Ingsoc, but to make all other modes of thought impossible." In other words, "a heretical thought—that is, a thought diverging from the principles of Ingsoc—should be literally unthinkable."

Here, in what we hope is only a terrifying fiction, Orwell shows the practical exploitation by a totalitarian state of this principle: Language shapes the thoughts of the speaker and his views of the world.

GEORGE ORWELL

The Principles of Newspeak*

Newspeak was the official language of Oceania and had been devised to meet the ideological needs of Ingsoc, or English Socialism. In the year 1984 there was not as yet anyone who used Newspeak as his sole means of communication, either in speech or writing. The leading articles in the Times were written in it, but this was a tour de force which could only be carried out by a specialist. It was expected that Newspeak would have finally superseded Oldspeak (or Standard English, as we should call it) by about the year 2050. Meanwhile it gained ground steadily, all Party members tending to use Newspeak words and grammatical constructions more and more in their everyday speech. The version in use in 1984, and embodied in the Ninth and Tenth Editions of the Newspeak dictionary, was a provisional one, and contained many superfluous words and archaic formations which were due to be suppressed later. It is with the final, perfected version, as embodied in the Eleventh Edition of the dictionary, that we are concerned here.

The purpose of Newspeak was not only to provide a medium of expression for the world-view and mental habits proper to the devotees of Ingsoc, but to make all other modes of thought impossible. It was intended that when Newspeak had been adopted once and for all and Oldspeak forgotten, a heretical thought —that is, a thought diverging from the principles of

* From *Nineteen Eighty-Four* by George Orwell. Copyright, 1947, by Harcourt, Brace and Company, Inc. Reprinted by permission of Harcourt, Brace and Company, Inc.

Ingsoc—should be literally unthinkable, at least so far as thought is dependent on words. Its vocabulary was so constructed as to give exact and often very subtle expression to every meaning that a Party member could properly wish to express, while excluding all other meanings and also the possibility of arriving at them by indirect methods. This was done partly by the invention of new words, but chiefly by eliminating undesirable words and by stripping such words as remained of unorthodox meanings, and so far as possible of all secondary meanings whatever. To give a single example. The word *free* still existed in Newspeak, but it could only be used in such statements as "This dog is free from lice" or "This field is free from weeds." It could not be used in its old sense of "politically free" or "intellectually free," since political and intellectual freedom no longer existed even as concepts, and were therefore of necessity nameless. Quite apart from the suppression of definitely heretical words, reduction of vocabulary was regarded as an end in itself, and no word that could be dispensed with was allowed to survive. Newspeak was designed not to extend but to *diminish* the range of thought, and this purpose was indirectly assisted by cutting the choice of words down to a minimum. . . . The expression of unorthodox opinions, above a very low level, was well-nigh impossible. It was of course possible to utter heresies of a very crude kind, a species of blasphemy. It would have been possible, for example, to say *Big Brother is ungood*. But this statement, which to an orthodox ear merely conveyed a self-evident absurdity, could not have been sustained by reasoned argument, because the necessary words were not available. Ideas inimical to Ingsoc could only be entertained in a vague wordless form, and could only be named in very broad terms which lumped together and condemned whole groups of heresies without defining them in doing so. One could, in fact, only use Newspeak for unorthodox purposes by illegitimately translating some of the words back into Oldspeak. For example, *All mans are equal* was a possible Newspeak sentence, but only in the same sense in which *All men are redhaired* is a possible Oldspeak sentence. It did not contain a grammatical error, but it expressed a palpable untruth, i.e., that all men are of equal size, weight, or strength. The concept of political equality no longer existed, and this secondary meaning had accordingly been purged out of the word *equal*. In 1984, when Oldspeak was still the normal means of communication, the danger theoretically existed that in using Newspeak words one might remember their original meanings. In practice it was not difficult for any person well grounded in *doublethink* to avoid doing this, but within a couple of generations even the possibility of such a lapse would have vanished. A person growing up with Newspeak as his sole language would no more know that *equal* had once had the secondary meaning of "politically equal," or that *free* had once meant "intellectually free," than, for instance, a person who had never heard of chess would be aware of the secondary meanings attaching to *queen* and *rook*. There would be many crimes and errors which it would be beyond his power to commit, simply because they were nameless and therefore unimaginable. And it was to be foreseen that with the passage of time the distinguishing characteristics of Newspeak would become more and more pronounced —its words growing fewer and fewer, their meanings more and more rigid, and the chance of putting them to improper uses always diminishing.

When Oldspeak had been once and for all superseded, the last link with the past would have been severed. History had already been rewritten, but fragments of the literature of the past survived here and there, imperfectly censored, and so long as one retained one's knowledge of Oldspeak it was possible to read them. In the future such fragments, even if they chanced to survive, would be unintelligible and untranslatable. It was impossible to translate any passage of Oldspeak into Newspeak unless it either referred to some technical process or some very simple everyday action, or was already orthodox (*goodthinkful* would be the Newspeak expression) in tendency. In practice this meant that no book written before approximately 1960 could be translated as a whole. Prerevolutionary literature could only be subjected to ideological translation—that is, alteration in sense as well as language. Take for example the well-known passage from the Declaration of Independence:

We hold these truths to be self-evident, that all men are created equal, that they are endowed by their Creator with certain inalienable rights, that among these are life, liberty and the pursuit of happiness. That to secure these rights, Governments are instituted among men, deriving their powers from the consent of the governed. That whenever any form of Government becomes destructive of those ends, it is the right of the People to alter or abolish it, and to institute new Government . . .

It would have been quite impossible to render this into Newspeak while keeping to the sense of the original. The nearest one could come to doing so would be to swallow the whole passage up in the single word *crimethink*. A full translation could only be an ideological translation, whereby Jefferson's words would be changed into a panegyric on absolute government.

A good deal of the literature of the past was, indeed, already being transformed in this way. Considerations of prestige made it desirable to preserve the memory of certain historical figures, while at the same time bringing their achievements into line with the philosophy of Ingsoc. Various writers, such as Shakespeare, Milton, Swift, Byron, Dickens, and some others were therefore in process of translation; when the task had been completed, their original writings, with all else that survived of the literature of the past, would be destroyed. These translations were a slow and difficult business, and it was not expected that they would be finished before the first or second decade of the twenty-first century. There were also large quantities of merely utilitarian literature—indispensable technical manuals and the like—that had to be treated in the same way. It was chiefly in order to allow time for the preliminary work of translation that the final adoption of Newspeak had been fixed for so late a date as 2050.

For at least a hundred years now, various groups have been at work devising artifical languages—fortunately for the human race not for the purpose of enslaving men, as Orwell's Newspeak was designed, but from the belief that a common language would lead the peoples of the world to exchange ideas, to grow to understand each other better and to value each other more, and to come to live together finally in peace.

In the following article, Robert A. Hall, Jr., professor of modern languages at Cornell University and author of *Melanesian Pidgin* and *Descriptive Italian Grammar,* reviews the various possibilities which might serve as a world language: Latin; some existing national language—French or English, for instance; one of the artificial languages—Interlingua, Volapük, Esperanto, or Ido, which Otto Jespersen advocated; some simplified version of a national language such as Melanesian Pidgin, or Ogden and Richards' Basic English, with its vocabulary of 850 words.

One by one, Hall discards each possibility, concluding that a world language is not only impossible, but also, as a matter of fact, even undesirable. "The problems besetting the world as a whole are non-linguistic," he writes, "and use of a single language would not help solve them in the slightest." Not every authority shares Hall's point of view, of course. For an answer to many of his criticisms, you will want to read Mario Pei's chapter "It Can Be Done!" in *The Story of Language.*

ROBERT A. HALL, JR.

One World, One Language?*

Ever since Biblical times people have been wishing that all mankind might talk the same language, so that—they've hoped—misunderstanding and quarrels and wars might not arise through failure of man to get what his neighbor was saying. . . .

There is a very good reason why interest and plans for a universal language have been intensified in modern times. We are decidedly worse off than were the Middle Ages. In those days there was one, and

* Reprinted from *Leave Your Language Alone!* by Robert A. Hall, Jr., by permission of *Linguistica.* Copyright 1950 by *Linguistica.*

only one, language used all throughout the West of Europe by intellectual men, for their thinking, writing, and communication: Latin. . . . And Latin had an intellectual tradition back of it, and extensive literature in religious and profane subjects of then current interest, which kept its use alive. Under these conditions—and only under these conditions—it was possible to keep Latin "alive" long after its popular developments, in the Romance tongues, had changed so far as to become independent languages. . . .

The chief alternative to use of a dead language is the adoption of some modern language as an international means of communication. . . . From about 1650 to 1750, France was the dominant nation of Europe politically and intellectually, and the fortunes of French as an international auxiliary language followed the fortunes of France. . . . English seems to have gradually been taking the place of French during the last two hundred years, due to first English and then American leadership in commerce, in industry, and science. . . . But in the last hundred and fifty years . . . nationalism has been growing ever stronger in almost all nations, large and small, and the people of each country have tended to use their own language as a symbol of their own nationality, the symbol . . . which they are least willing to give up. . . .

Then . . . why not get a language that will not be connected with any specific nation and that therefore will not cause antagonism on that score? . . . For the last hundred years or more, many people have been fascinated by such an idea, and it has been estimated that over a hundred such artificial languages have been invented—averaging something like a language a year. Their inventors have given them all sorts of names, like Interlingua, Kosmos, Occidental, Parla, Spokil, Universala, and so forth. The three most successful to date have been Volapük, Esperanto, and Ido, of which the best known of all is undoubtedly the second. . . .

Esperanto and similar languages have essentially failed to catch on, however, for much the same reasons we pointed out for Latin. In the first place, as soon as they come to be spoken by any sizeable number of people, they automatically start to change—whether unintentionally, due to the influence of the native language of each speaker and to internal organic change, or intentionally, as in the case of the reform made by the Idoists. . . . There are so few native speakers of Esperanto that they are not enough to serve as a standard of usage. And there is no body of material, oral or written, to serve as a canon, such as there is in classical Latin or Greek, or such as naturally grows out of the situation for any living language.

Recently, another group—the International Auxiliary Language Association, or IALA—has begun an ambitious program for the construction of still another auxiliary language of this kind. . . . The Iala language, when made available, may have a slightly more scientific basis to its choice of material than Esperanto or Ido; but, so far as can be told at this stage, it will be the same kind of pick-and-choose affair. . . .

Another objection to all the artificial auxiliary languages that have been constructed so far, is that they are essentially designed by and for West Europeans. A language like Esperanto, although supposedly simplified from our point of view, still keeps the essential parts of speech (noun, adjective, verb, etc.) of

Indo-European, and the concepts and categories of meaning that our languages have made us familiar with. A speaker of—say—Chinese or Telugu or some American Indian language would have as much difficulty with the sounds, forms, and thought pattern of Esperanto as he would with those of French or English or German. . . .

A still further solution is . . . to try to make a simplified version of some national language already spoken. . . . The resulting "minimum language" is called a *pidgin*. Pidgin languages have developed in great number, especially those based on Portuguese, French, and English; just to limit ourselves to pidgin English, there are varieties of pidgin spoken in China, West Africa, Melanesia, and Australia. Most people have the idea that a pidgin language is just a jargon, a hash, a "corruption" without any rules or grammar, spoken the way an ignorant American might try to talk to a Chinese laundryman. This is a wholly mistaken idea. Pidgin English, although reduced in grammar and vocabulary from its base, has nevertheless a true linguistic structure of its own and is a language in its own right—but one which has gone its own way. . . . Interesting changes of meaning have taken place, and some words have been greatly extended beyond their original English use, in a way which is perhaps superficially amusing to speakers of English, but which has its own logic and sense. Thus, we're likely to be amused at first when we find that "hair" is expressed by *gras bilong hed*, literally "the grass of the head" (*bilong* is a preposition, meaning "of" or "for"). But, when we consider that the natives knew the words *gras* "grass" and *hed* "head," it was the most logical thing in the world to compare the hair to grass growing out of the head, and easier to make the phrase *gras bilong hed* than to learn a completely new and separate word for "hair." In the same way, in Melanesian Pidgin the word *ars*, originally "buttocks," has had its meaning extended to cover any kind of "bottom"—for instance, *ars bilong diwai* means "the bottom of the tree.". . .

But makers of reduced versions of modern major languages do not seem to have wanted to bother with pidgin languages. . . . The best known of these reduced languages is of course Ogden and Richards' *Basic English*. This language is strictly limited in vocabulary to 850 words . . . plus 18 special auxiliary verbs or "operators" such as *get, do, be,* etc. Ordinary English spelling is used, and little attention has been paid to the phonetic side of the problem; apparently it was assumed that foreigners' difficulties in learning English nouns were of little or no weight, and the language seems to have been envisaged primarily as a means of written communication. Although the number of individual words is limited to 850, the number of compounds and combinations in which they may be used—in ordinary English patterns—is enormous; so, as Basic English uses the separate words *fancy, dress,* and *ball* (in all the different meanings which standard English attaches to those words), it is permissible to use also the combination of *fancy dress ball*. Hence, despite its professed limitations of 850 words, the actual number of possible combinations, and the range of meaning covered by Basic English vocabulary is very great, and all according to the patterns of standard English. . . . The choice of the 850 words of the Basic English vocabulary is quite arbitrary, and includes such a relatively unimportant term as *sticky*, while omitting others that would be far more serviceable. The meanings, both literary and transferred, are simply those of ordinary English vocabulary, without regard to the fact that for speakers of most other languages, our range of meaning for any particular word would be quite unheard of: the speaker of Russian, for instance, would never find it natural to speak of the *leg* of a table or the *foot* of a mountain. . . . The auxiliary verbs or "operators" constitute one of the hardest parts of Basic English for any non-speaker of English, since such words as *get* and *do* are among the trickiest things in the English language. In short, Basic English is quite without the ease and simplicity that has been claimed for it. . . .

Well, then what is the answer, after all? A dead language won't work; nor will a completely artificial language; . . . nor will a naive and unskillful reduction of a major language. We might perhaps think of making a better job of reducing a major language, taking lessons from Pidgin English and trying to see in what way our language could be reduced and simplified to make it usable by people of other speech. The trouble is, we would have to not only . . . reduce its phonemes, forms, and constructions drastically, but also change the range of meanings of its words, in such a way that it would be almost unrecognizable to speakers of English itself, and incur their hostility and rejection in much the same way that Pidgin English does. There's no way out along that path, either. . . .

When we look at the whole quest for an international language, we notice one thing above all others: the desire for *ease* in learning, an ease greater than that of learning an ordinary major language. . . . [Yet] it seems likely that ease of acquisition can be gained only at the cost of impoverishment of form or content. Although a pidgin language is a perfectly workable and usable form of communication, and you can convey in Melanesian Pidgin, say, any idea that you can in standard English, it often takes longer to do so just because of the limited means; what you gain in simplicity, you lose in richness and directness of expression. . . .

Furthermore, the difficulty of acquiring another language is something which has been greatly exaggerated. . . . Greater "ease" of learning an artificial or reduced auxiliary language, we now see, is something largely illusory, and certainly not worth the price in loss of communicative power as contrasted with a real language.

Then why not all agree on some one language as *the* language for the "one world" which many of us have yearned for, and everybody learn that language at least as a second language, with the hope that perhaps eventually the whole world might shift to it as a first language? I confess to having entertained such notions at one time. . . . Yet it is an impossibility, after all. Even if we could reach some ideal condition where nationalistic feelings did not preclude adoption of some one national language as a world means of communication, we still could never attain world linguistic unity. To attain and keep linguistic unity, the whole human race would have to be much more capable of accepting and following rigid rules—in regard to all aspects of language: sounds, grammar, vocabulary, meanings, and even spelling—than they are or give any sign of becoming. As the chosen language became more and more widespread, it would automatically be differentiated into dialects, since it would be learned in somewhat different form and adapted somewhat differently by the speakers of each different language. These dialects would soon move farther and farther from each other, both through internal organic change and through borrowing from each other, until after a few centuries we would simply have another set of different languages again—and the whole problem of translation, foreign language learning, etc., would start in over again.

Furthermore, hasn't the problem perhaps been ascribed to the wrong causes? Those who advocate an international language usually assume—whether they say so or not—that misunderstandings and international quarrels and wars are *caused* by differences in language. . . . There have been plenty of instances in which people of the same language have fought each other bitterly and long: just think of our Revolutionary War, our Civil War, all the wars between different countries in Latin America in which both sides speak Spanish, or the religious wars in almost every European country in the sixteenth century. On the other hand, we can see from the example of Switzerland that speakers of four national languages (French, German, Italian, and Rhaeto-Romance) can live together and get along extremely well, on the whole, in one nation, and in a rather cramped and restricted territory, at that. The Swiss get along together, neither because of nor in spite of their linguistic diversity, but because they have common interests in the economic and political and cultural sphere—in non-linguistic matters, in short—that they are willing to take the trouble to cooperate about. The conditions for peace and harmony are essentially non-linguistic in nature; two people of almost identical speech can hate each other to the point of strife and murder, whereas two people of completely different speech can get along well enough to cooperate whole-heartedly.

The whole international language question, then—the idea that, to have "one world," we must of necessity have one language, and the debate over how to attain and spread that one language—is illusory, and based on an unrealistic assumption to begin with. We do not need linguistic unity in order to attain world peace. . . . We will still continue to need more than one language, both for everyday use in our own communities, and for international use; and the present major internationally used languages (English, French, Spanish, German and—more and more—Russian, Chinese, Arabic, Malay) are perfectly satisfactory for the purpose. Besides, the variety of languages spoken throughout the world is an asset to the human race as well as, or perhaps even more than, a liability; for, after all, a language is one way of organizing and classifying human experience, and we certainly have no right to say that our ways of organizing and classifying human experience have reached such perfection that we can afford to throw out all but our own. Multilingualism is with us to stay, in short, and there are good reasons for not regarding it as a curse and trying to get out of it, but, quite the contrary, for accepting it as a blessing and trying to turn it to our best advantage.

Not to be taken too seriously, of course, the following article by Alden H. Smith supports Hall's argument that Basic English is essentially unsatisfactory. Inter-

jections do not come out the same in English, Russian, Spanish, and Japanese—and of what use is a world language if a man cannot say "ouch," or something, in it?

(Alden H. Smith served as an army French and German interpreter during the Second World War and is vice president of the Magazine Institute.)

ALDEN H. SMITH

Basic Basic*

What I cannot understand about Basic English is why Mr. I. A. Richards, the inventor or discoverer, never thought to supply it with an "ouch," "kerplunk," or a "for gosh sakes." It does seem pretty obvious that situations demanding these words are just as frequent as those in which "and," "but," or "cat" is sufficient.

I imagine Mr. Richards fell into the common error of supposing *everybody* says "ouch" when hurt and "plop" when trying to describe the impact of a small object falling into a liquid medium. Nothing could be further from the truth. Just let Mr. Richards try calling a Portuguese cat by the kitty-kitty-kitty method. That cat will remain unmoved until Richards translates into Portuguese thus: "Biz-biz-biz!"

And so it is with all those other little words which the grammarians call interjections, onomatopoeic words, or which they ignore altogether. We take it for granted that bells in all countries say "ding-dong" and that "ow" and "ouch" are *essential* expressions of pain; yet every nationality has its own repertory.

Let us, for example, imagine a Russian carpenter

* Reprinted from "Basic Basic" by Alden H. Smith by permission of the author.

banging his thumb with a hammer. In Basic English he would be tongue-tied or confined to some such silly remark as "I have just brought the hammer down upon my thumb." Given access to his native vocabulary he would start out with an anguished "Oi—oi!" I think that he would then call the manufacturer of the hammer a lousy "sookin sin," but that's getting away from simple interjections.

I should mention here that Ivan also had a Spanish assistant, José Maria Gutierrez y Zumbamba. The moment the hammer landed on Ivan's thumb this José began to chuckle, "¡Je! ¡Je! ¡Je!" and then, his carburetor flooded with exclamation points and unable to contain himself, he burst right out with a loud "¡Ja! ¡Ja! ¡Ja!"

Don't think for a minute that the Russians are overburdened with any great love of humanity. If the positions had been reversed and it had been the Spaniard's thumb that got whacked, it would have been José's turn to make a Spanish "ouch" like this, "¡Huy!" and Ivan would have clapped his hands to his ribs and roared, "Xa—xa—xa!" which the Russians consider to be laughter.

But it was Ivan's thumb, so instead of "Xa—xa—xa!" he spits out in disgust, "Foo!" Irritated by José's laughter he then changes the "Foo!" to an angry "Tfoo!" (This is one of those nuances of the Russian language which make it such a flexible medium for the exchange of ideas.)

José counters with a defiant "¡Puf!"

The Russian backs down in the face of the fiery Spaniard. "Ookh!" he whimpers in abject fear.

So José decides to chuck the job—mañana he can get another one—and he saunters off calling his dog to his side, "¡Tus! ¡Tus! ¡Tus!" Head in the clouds, he falls right into a freshly prepared batch of cement, "¡Cataplum!" It serves him right and gives us a chance to replace him with a Japanese assistant carpenter.

Instead of pushing a Japanese saw through the plank you *pull* it. And there may be something funny about the hammers, too, so we had better imagine that Mr. Nakayama is provided with a Western-style hammer.

Well, Nakayama throws himself into the work with the old samurai spirit of *Yamato-damashii* and to hell with halfway measures. First thing you know, *he* bangs his thumb and screws his face up in pain. "Sah!" he groans; or "Mah!" or "Oya!" or "Eh!" or "Oya—mah!" It doesn't seem to matter which, since they can all mean "ouch." "Sah," depending on the context, may sometimes be translated as just a thoughtful "Hmm—" or an "Ugh!" of disgust or a negative "Unh—unh!"—or, as in this instance, as "Oh, I've mashed my goddam thumb!" It is thus very difficult to know what the Japanese are thinking or feeling just by listening to them. They are said to be inscrutable. Believe me, if we said "Pow!" or "Zowie!" or "Boing!" interchangeably for all occasions, we could be considered every bit as mysterious.

From these few examples on a single construction job it is clear there is no international unity in interjections. Bells ring variously in all tongues—"Din—don—din," "Tlimtlom," and so forth. Rattle a stick along a French picket fence and the fence gives out with a "Rataplan." And who can say what is the correct formula for calling a Siamese cat or what strange syllable means "Sic 'em!" to an Afghan hound?

It would certainly seem to behoove Mr. I. A. Richards to start at the beginning next time and give us something down to earth. I just wonder what Mr. Richards would say in his vaunted Basic if he should come home some day and trip and fall over his French poodle or slip on a Persian scatter rug.

part II

Wherein Are Introduced Standard
Makers and Problems of Conformity

Word Men

Many men have thought the use of language important enough to spend their lives trying to give us the means of improving communication. A look at the lives of some of these men will perhaps aid us in understanding what they had in mind.

"In many respects this Yankee schoolmaster is a far more appropriate symbol of our young nation than is either the cosmopolite printer-philosopher Franklin or the squirish-minded Washington." In these words Thomas Pyles, professor of English at the University of Florida, summarizes the influence of Noah Webster, the American lexicographer whose piety and moral earnestness did as much to form American attitudes as his dictionary and speller did to standardize American speech.

THOMAS PYLES

Noah Webster, Man and Symbol*

Noah Webster, whose name is known all over the English-speaking world—"according to Webster" is as

* From *Words and Ways of American English* by Thomas Pyles, copyright 1952 by Random House, Inc. Reprinted by permission of Random House, Inc.

167

familiar a recommendation as "according to Hoyle" —was a Connecticut Yankee whose father, a thrifty and industrious farmer, ultimately rose to the rank and dignities of a Calvinist deacon. It is worthy of note, to show the superior moral background of our great American schoolmaster, that the senior Webster, also named Noah, once served as one of a committee appointed to reprimand a harassed pastor for tippling. The younger Noah grew up with all the tiresome virtues. He was possessed of almost unlimited determination and an infinite capacity for taking pains. He rose early, worked hard, took healthful exercise, was strictly temperate, led the church choir on Sundays, and, full of years, honors, and virtues, lived to the venerable age of eighty-five. The lovable qualities which we detect in the great English lexicographer, even despite the frequent waspishness of Boswell's portrayal—the bohemianism, the fondness for late hours and conviviality, the endearing eccentricities, the prejudices (so often justified), the very human passionateness, the brilliant talk, the warmth of the transcendent smile which every so often lighted up his ugly, pitted face—all these were absent in the Great Cham of the American language, who had none of the vast personal charm which is so striking a characteristic of Dr. Johnson. Webster was smug, self-assured, and pugnacious in his pedantry as in his Puritanism and his patriotism: the dour, thin-lipped, jut-jawed righteousness of his later portraits seem always to have been characteristic of him. It is difficult to think of him as ever having been young; the report of the mild foppishness of his college days surprises the chronicler when he comes upon it.

But there was the stuff of greatness in him. Furthermore, he possessed the capacity to work twice as long and hard as other men without getting tired. His moral earnestness drove him to toil indefatigably for the greater glory of God, of his beloved country, and of Noah Webster. In many respects this Yankee schoolmaster is a far more appropriate symbol of our young nation than is either the cosmopolite printer-philosopher Franklin or the squirish-minded Washington. . . .

In the preface to his first lexicographical work, A *Compendious Dictionary of the English Language* (1806), Webster announced that his intention had been to compile a dictionary "which shall exhibit a far more correct state of the language than any work of this kind." Having given up some of his more fantastic spelling reforms, he now predicted that, because of printing, mutual intercourse would continue to exist between English-speaking peoples; "but those terms in Great Britain which express local ideas only will be lost in the dialects of India and America, while local circumstances among the descendants of the English in their new settlements will originate new words or give to old words new significations which will never be received or generally known in Great Britain." He was furthermore convinced that "in each of the countries peopled by Englishmen, a distinct dialect of the language will gradually be formed, the principal of which will be that of the United States.". . .

The years between the publication of the *Compendious Dictionary* and 1825 were largely devoted to the preparation of *An American Dictionary of the English Language*, though the indefatigable Webster found time to engage in political activities, give pious but unsought advice to President-elect Madison, and become a founder of Amherst College.

Unlike the earlier lexicographical work, which provided only spelling, pronunciation, and definition, this was to be an etymological dictionary, and Webster early set about to prepare himself for the great task—in his opinion not merely to set down a record of the language, but "to search for truth, to proscribe error, and repress anomaly." Even with such exalted ideals, however, it was necessary to have some information at hand, and he set about to prepare a synopsis of the supposed affinities of the twenty-three languages, not to mention "the early dialects of English and German," which he is supposed to have learned.

Moving about an especially constructed semicircular desk, thumbing grammars and dictionaries, noting similarities and supposed correspondences of consonants and letting the vowels fall where they may, is not the same thing as buckling down and actually learning languages. Webster might have saved himself a great deal of time if he had taken the trouble to find out what keener-minded and better informed men had discovered instead of pursuing such feckless tasks as trying to prove, in line with his belief in the divine origin of language, that "Chaldee" (Biblical Aramaic) was the parent of all languages. He did not bother to learn Sanskrit, the study of which in the late eighteenth century gave rise to the Indo-European hypothesis, namely, the now universal assumption of a common ancestor for most of the languages spoken in Europe and the Americas, as well as some spoken in Asia, the Indic and the Iranian. Why the discoveries of Sir William Jones were not better known to him—Jones had written forty years before the publication of the *American Dictionary*—it is impossible to say. The foundations of modern linguistic science had been soundly laid by such scholars as Jones, Jacob Grimm, Franz Bopp, and Friedrich von Schlegel. But Webster was too busy "mastering" languages—according to his own claims, German, Dutch, Swedish, Danish, Anglo-Saxon, Gothic, Welsh, Armoric (Breton), "Hyberne" (Irish), Ethiopic, Persian, Hebrew, Samaritan, Chaldaic, Syriac, Arabic, Greek, Latin, Italian, Spanish, French, Portuguese, and Russian—to familiarize himself with the important and exciting discoveries which others had made and which were by no means unknown in this country. James Gates Percival, the poet, who read proof on the American Dictionary, was quite familiar with them, but Webster would not listen to the young man's remonstrances. Those "Chaldee" etymologies were very dear to his heart. . . .

As an etymologist Webster was something less than adequate. As has already been pointed out, he chose to ignore (perhaps because of an inability to read German, one of those twenty-three languages he is reported to have "mastered") the really significant work which had been done in linguistics in his day, preferring the tower of Babel explanation of the origin of individual tongues to the scientific methods of the Indo-Europeanists. Furthermore, he does not seem really to have learned languages at all well. Charlton Laird in his "Etymology, Anglo-Saxon, and Noah Webster" (*American Speech*, February, 1946) concludes that Webster's knowledge of Anglo-Saxon (Old English) was inferior to that of Thomas Jefferson, who claimed to be no better than an amateur. Professor Laird has examined four works in Old English which Webster presented to Yale in 1837, presumably the only ones in this older form of our language that he owned. From marginal notes in Webster's hand—the sort, according to Laird, which "one would expect from a beginning graduate student"—it is obvious that Webster's ignorance of Old English was deplorable as compared with what was well known by British scholars in his day. In the light of such facts, it is difficult not to question his proficiency in some of the other languages which he "mastered" in the course of a myriad half-circuits around his famous desk. In any case, subsequent editors have without comment excised by the basketful Webster's etymological "boners."

But if his etymologies are frequently worse than worthless, there can be no doubt that Webster was superb in definition, though even here his personal bias is frequently evident. In the *Compendious Dictionary* he has defined *Federalist* as "a friend to the Constitution of the U. States," paralleling Johnson's definition of a Tory as "one who adheres to the ancient constitution of the state, and the apostolical hierarchy of the Church of England, opposed to a Whig." The *American Dictionary* also contains a good many nonobjective definitions and illustrations designed to support the Calvinistic department of the Christian religion. But such definitions are, after all, exceptional, just as are the oftquoted crotchety definitions of Johnson. For the most part, the reader is struck with admiration and must perforce agree with Sir James Murray, the great editor of the *Oxford English Dictionary*, that Webster was "a born definer of words."

Unquestionably the most pungent, choleric, witty, and eccentric lexicographer of the English language was Samuel Johnson (1709–1784), whose position of "literary dictator" in eighteenth-century England was unchallenged. He was much more than a compiler of dictionaries and a writer who detested the labor entailed in the art of writing. His dictionary in itself is almost enough to indicate the paradoxical nature of the man: humorous, logical, prejudiced in politics and religion, reasonable, and, as occasion demanded, vituperative.

Johnson's dictionary was one of the first studies of English as a living language, most preceding English dictionaries being attempts to compile English equivalents for Latin words. Consequently errors of definition were inevitable. But any person who has struggled for the right word will be cheered by the forthright reasonableness of Johnson's answer to a lady who asked him why he had incorrectly defined *pastern* as "the knee of a horse": "Sheer ignorance, Madam!"

GEORGE B. WOODS, HOMER A. WYATT, AND
GEORGE K. ANDERSON

From The Dictionary*

When Johnson defined *lexicographer* as "a harmless drudge," he spoke from experience as well as from a sense of humor. The *Dictionary* occupied his time and thought for eight years or more, but it was a remarkable achievement, since during the period he was busy with much other writing.

As stated in the original "Plan," addressed to Lord Chesterfield, it was Johnson's hope to write "a dic-

* From *The Literature of England*, single volume edition, by Woods, Wyatt, and Anderson. Copyright, 1953, by Scott, Foresman and Company, and reprinted with their permission.

tionary by which the pronunciation of our language may be fixed, and its attainment facilitated, by which its purity may be preserved, its use ascertained, and its duration lengthened." Although adhering tenaciously to these fixed standards, Johnson later admitted in the Preface that language is subject to change, yet his work is significant in that it established the criterion of reputable use. The *Dictionary*, therefore, was meant to aid the writer rather than the reader of the English language. In his ambitious way Johnson set out to include quotations illustrating the proper uses of words defined. This feature was an innovation in dictionary making and one of priceless value in any survey of the language. In still another feature the *Dictionary* is a notable work. Johnson excelled in definitions. Sometimes a delicious flavor was given by odd quirks of personal prejudice or humor, or by difficulties encountered in explaining the obvious. With little etymological understanding, he safely relied upon his abundant common sense and his keen, vigorous intellect to carry him through the project. The chief merit of the *Dictionary* lies in its definitions; not only do they illustrate Johnson's personality but they throw much light upon the eighteenth-century English Tory as well.

dry: desiccative.

dryness: siccity or aridity.

excise: a hateful tax levied upon commodities, and adjudged, not by the common judges of property, but wretches hired by those to whom excise is paid.

Grub Street: the name of a street in London, much inhabited by writers of small histories, *dictionaries,* and temporary poems; whence any mean production is called Grub Street.

hatchet-faced: an ugly face;

such, I suppose, as might be hewn out of a block by a hatchet.

lexicographer: a writer of dictionaries, a harmless drudge that busies himself in tracing the original and detailing the significance of words.

network: anything reticulated or decussated at equal distances with interstices between the intersections.

oats: a grain which in England is generally given to horses, but in Scotland supports the people.

patriotism: the last refuge of a scoundrel.

patron: one who countenances, supports, or protects. Commonly a wretch who supports with insolence, and is paid with flattery.

pension: an allowance made to anyone without an equivalent. In England it is generally understood to mean pay given to a state hireling for treason to his country.

pensioner: a slave of state, hired by a stipend to obey his master.

politician: a man of artifice; one deep of contrivance.

Redcoat: a name of contempt for a soldier.

thunder: a most bright flame rising on a sudden, moving with great violence, and with a very rapid velocity, through the air, according to any determination, and commonly ending with a loud noise or rattling.

Tory: one who adheres to the ancient constitution of the state, and the apostolical hierarchy of the Church of England, opposed to a Whig.

transpire: to escape from secrecy to notice, a sense lately innovated from France without necessity.

Whig: the name of a faction.

willow: a tree worn by forlorn lovers.

Though his compilation of English synonyms and antonyms may be responsible for clichés "imbedded in the numbed minds" of its readers, Roget has exerted other, and perhaps happier, influences through at least ten million copies of his *Thesaurus.* Charles Poore, co-

editor of the *Books of the Times,* in noting Roget's
175th natal anniversary (January 18, 1954) points out
some of these influences and gives a brief biography of
the thesaurist whose work has become a prop, crutch,
or tool, as the writer's discrimination may determine.

CHARLES POORE

Birthday (Natal Day, Jubilee)*

A distinguished British doctor of Swiss descent
called (named, styled, known as, and, of course,
yclept) Peter Mark Roget, whose 175th birthday
(anniversary, natal day, jubilee) will be celebrated
(honored, commemorated, hallowed) tomorrow,
ranks high among the movers and shakers (savants,
freaks, fools and men of destiny) who have shaped
the utterances (speeches, declarations, books, plays
and advertising) of the wildly wordy modern world.

Ten million copies, at a conservative estimate, of
Roget's immortal "Thesaurus of English Words and
Phrases" and its progeny are loose today on the face
of creation. How many clichés they have imbedded
in the numbed minds of men and women no one
can estimate; how many arrowy phrases they have
sped none can tell. You will find a Roget—or one of
its variants—in every library and publishing house and
city room, on the desks of scholars and statesmen
and their scribbling ghosts, the table of the cross-
word puzzle fanatic and the playwright or novelest
frantically seeking a fresh way to have a character
say: "We can't go on like this—something's got to
happen."

* Reprinted from "Birthday (Natal Day, Jubilee)" by Charles
Poore in *The New York Times Magazine,* January 17, 1954, by
permission of the author and of *The New York Times Magazine.*

In some quarters Roget's book is regarded somewhat like a bathtub: everybody likes to have it, few enjoy being seen using it. That's human enough. You can't expect a politician who has just fired a salvo of brilliant hints on salvation to the American people to add, in a quick aside: "I owe the phrasing to Roget." Or a celebrated writer, on being praised for the magnificently touching love scene in his latest success, to trace a pattern in the carpet with a diffident toe and say: "Shucks. As a matter of fact I got most of the words out of sections 865.1 (love n. *desire*), 894.3 (love n. *compliments*) and 897 (love n. *affection*) in my new thesaurus."

However, the thesaurus (dictionary, glossary, lexicon or gradus) also has earned its share of compliments. William Allen White called his Roget "a guide and ever-present help in trouble." The late Dr. Frank Crane, a formidable necromancer of words, once roundly asserted that it was "the chiefest tool of all writing craftsmen"—though purists suggested that he should open the book again and try to find something to replace that fearful "chiefest." And Hendrik Willem Van Loon harassed the publishers of one Roget version so overwhelmingly with suggestions for additions and changes that they dedicated the next edition to him. A noted editorial writer answered a query as to whether he used Roget by saying: "Well, I did, when I was learning the language."

An American novelist said last week that he used "Roget and whisky—usually in moderation." Another gave the familiar answer to the effect that he owned a copy but seldom opened it. A diplomatic attaché said he had one in his office in South America "to help me make my reports longer." Three newspaper editors gave different answers. One said he deplored Roget because he thought the use of a thesaurus fossilized writing. Another said he used Roget professionally and also for light reading. The third asked: What for? Does Roget tell you how to say: "Queen Mary's passengers carry own baggage in widespread pier tie-up," or "Millions throng Coney's sands as city swelters in record heat"? Lit'ry critics are apparently content with their own screechy adjectives.

If Peter Mark Roget (1779–1869) had not enjoyed an amazing longevity, the world would never have seen his thesaurus. Up to the time he was 70 he was far too busy being an eminent personage in British medicine and public affairs to whittle away hours editing one of the great best-sellers of all times.

Roget was the only son of a Swiss clergyman who presided over the French Protestant Church near the Bank of England in London's Threadneedle Street. His father died in 1783 when Peter was 4; his mother, the sister of Sir Samuel Romilly, brought him up in England and Scotland. At Edinburgh University he survived a practical immersion in medicine that included an attack of typhus fever and was graduated as an M.D. at 19.

In the bright gloom of pre-Victorian England he stood out as a Renaissance man. He was one of the founders of the Northern Dispensary, and served it without pay for many years. He lectured widely on medical matters and was an authority on epidemics. The government commissioned him to make a study of metropolitan London's water supply, unhampered by any notion that shooting chemical pellets into the air would cause copious rainfall. However, he invented a slide rule.

The slide rule, involving the logarithms of logarithms to an appalling degree, so impressed the members of the Royal Society that they elected Roget a
fellow in 1815, the year of Waterloo. Twelve years
later he became secretary of that society and helped
to launch another, the Society for the Diffusion of
Useful Knowledge, for which he wrote usefully
informing papers on electricity, galvanism and mag-
netism. He was also a fellow of the Royal College of
Physicians, a founder of London University and—by
now—no one will be astonished to hear that he spent
some time trying to build a calculating machine.

All through these years he was making a collection
of words and phrases arranged as methodically as
botanists classify plants. But this was for his private
use, mainly in his own publications, such as a paper
on the "Optical Deception in the Appearance of the
Spokes of a Wheel Seen Through Vertical Aper-
tures."

"I had, in the year 1805," he recalled in 1852 when
the first edition of his book appeared, "completed a
classed catalogue of words on a small scale, but on
the same principle, and nearly in the same form, as
the Thesaurus now published. I had often, during
that long interval found this little collection, scanty
and imperfect as it was, of much use to me in literary
composition, and often contemplated its extension
and improvement; but a sense of the magnitude of
the task, amidst a multitude of other avocations, de-
terred me from the attempt."

Roget was well aware that he was not the first man
who had entered the field (indeed, even Dr. Johnson's
friend, Mrs. Thrale, had been a Kilroy among the
thesauri), but he felt he had something useful to

offer; as usual, he meant to serve mankind. In a passage not without nobility, he said:

"A misapplied or misapprehended term is sufficient to give rise to fierce and interminable disputes; a misnomer has turned the tide of popular opinion; a verbal sophism has decided a party question; an artful watch-word, thrown among combustible materials, has kindled the flame of deadly warfare, and changed the destiny of an empire."

Roget's triumph and his tragedy was, ironically, that he himself was misunderstood. And that was inevitable for three reasons. First, because he made his infinitely systematic arrangement of words to fit ideas too complex. Many readers in search of a quick solution to their hazy intellectual problems never really learn how to use it. Second, because most readers absolutely refused to believe the book was not merely a dictionary of synonyms ("it is hardly possible to find two words having in all respects the same meaning," he said) and so encouraged the editors of many later versions of his book to sail somewhat falsely under the colors of Roget. Third, because the book seemed to cater to the eternal human hope for easy self-improvement, and thus became eternally popular.

Today, half a dozen different publishers are selling so many different books with the magic word "Roget" in the title that what may finally be needed is a thesaurus of Rogets. Each one has its own admirable features; each proclaims its homogenized virtues and white walled tires; a minority still pay royalty to the descendants of Roget in England. And yet, on balance, they all do less harm than good. They all shed light. They all provide introductions, for those who will take them, to the wonder and mysteries of words.

Roget himself died in 1869, in his ninety-first year, having seen his book pass through more than twenty English editions as well as others produced in America without what you could call his full concurrence. He was still revising his own version when he died, still working on a problem in communication between human beings that may be ultimately insoluble. For, as Winston Churchill once said in another connection: "We are divided by a common language."

Some editions of Roget's *Thesaurus* contain more than roots, stems, prefixes, affixes, synonyms, and antonyms. This fact became apparent to John Sack, after a careful study of his own copy. With a straight face he directs sly humor at the editor's selections of illustrative material.

JOHN SACK

Buy Your Synonyms in the Convenient Family Size*

Yma Sumac, the Peruvian girl who sings as low as Nelson Eddy and as high as almost anyone, is not a close friend of mine, but we are on the best of terms. We met in Cambridge, Massachusetts, a few years ago, and chatted awhile in Quechua, her native language, I saying "*Yeru yauri kocha urkko*" ("Ice needle lake mountain"), a few words I picked up in Peru and the only Quechua I know, and Miss Sumac replying, as nearly as I could tell, "*Rhubarb rhubarb*

* © 1954 The New Yorker Magazine, Inc.

rhubarb." Unhappily, our friendship never got past these two sentences, such as they were. We had reached an impasse. Miss Sumac, I sensed, was a bit perplexed, and my own Quechua was exhausted. I went home, a few minutes later, pretty much down in the mouth. That evening, however, I decided to write her, in English, about the whole affair. I wanted to say I was down in the mouth, or dejected, or saddened, but none of these seemed to be right, and, as usual, I reached for my copy of Roget's Thesaurus. My Thesaurus is the one in dictionary form, edited by Dr. C. O. Sylvester Mawson and published in 1931 by G. P. Putnam's Sons. It is a sober, workmanlike reference book, but its entry under "dejected," I discovered, was rather strange:

dejected, downcast, dispirited, disheartened, despondent, low-spirited, crestfallen, cowed, discouraged, heavy-hearted, sick, sick at heart, out of heart (or spirits), down in the mouth (colloq.), down on one's luck (colloq.), weary, downhearted (*with memories of Tommy Atkins in the black months of the World War: "Are we downhearted?" —NO!*).

The words in italics surprised me a good deal. Roget's Thesaurus, I felt, was hardly the place for memorials. I esteem Tommy Atkins as much as anyone does, but if Putnam's wished to commemorate him, I thought, it should have done so in one of its other titles—"History of Europe 1815–1923," for example, or "How to Like an Englishman," by C. V. R. Thompson.

All this, as I said, happened some time ago, and it didn't come to mind again till last week. Then, while writing to the editor of a local newspaper, I needed a synonym for the word "error," and when I looked into Roget's Thesaurus, I found an entry that was even more surprising:

error, fallacy, misconception, misapprehension, misunderstanding, aberration, obliquity, erroneousness, inexactness, fallaciousness . . . clerical error, bull, solecism, Malapropism, Spoonerism (*accidental transposition made famous by the Rev. W. A. Spooner of Oxford: "I am sorry to learn that you have been tasting your worms of late," said he to an undergraduate; "we all have a half-warmed fish in our bosoms;" "I have just received a blushing crow;" "for real enjoyment give me a well-boiled icycle." Asked if he sang, Mr. Spooner said: "I know only two tunes—'God Save the Weasel' and 'Pop Goes the Queen.'" Spooner certainly added to the joy of nations.*)

Now, it seemed to me that one example, if any, would have been enough. And what's this about the "joy of nations"? Dr. Mawson's opinion of the Reverend Dr. Spooner, I thought, scarcely belonged in a book of synonyms. (Besides, I cannot see how Spooner added joy to any nations but England, Australia, the United States, and a very few others, since blushing crows and half-warmed fish are surely lost in translation.)

By now I was curious about these ad libs and asides in Roget's Thesaurus, and I went through the book, page by page, to see if there were more. I discovered only two or three. One of them, under "oracle," was in the form of a question:

oracle, prophet, prophetess (*fem.*), seer, seeress (*fem.*), sibyl, soothsayer, augur, diviner, haruspex . . . weather forecaster, meteorologist (*dare we include him among the prophets?*)

Another ad lib came under the general heading of "instrument":

lever, crow, crowbar, jimmy or jemmy (*usually in sections for the burglar's convenience*)

Why did Dr. Mawson choose to give us this bit of information? I, for one, had no idea. I found a hint, however, in the preface, where Dr. Mawson, speaking of the Thesaurus, said, "simplicity is the keynote, the convenience of the consulter being always kept in mind." Dr. Mawson, in listing the synonyms for "lever," seems to have kept in mind the convenience of burglars. It is possible, I suppose, that the consulters of Roget's Thesaurus include a small but loyal group of burglars, who will be convenienced to know that a jimmy, or jemmy, is built in sections. In the same way, an after-dinner speaker would be convenienced by the handy list of Spoonerisms, and a phrase like "Are we downhearted? NO!" could prove very convenient, at times, to a captain of infantry. What puzzles me, then, is why Dr. Mawson paid mind to the convenience of infantry captains, burglars, and after-dinner speakers while neglecting that of, say, ordinary businessmen. Why didn't he include, for them, a listing like this:

guaranty, guarantee, assurance, insurance, warranty, engagement, undertaking agreement, contract, covenant; pledge, vadium, collateral, earnest, stake, deposit, pawn, bail, gage, tie; debenture, bond, stock (*Consolidated Edison is now selling at 45 3/4.*)

If Dr. Mawson wants his Thesaurus to be as convenient to most people as it presumably is to burglars, he will have to do a great deal of revision. According to the preface, Thesaurus readers include the "leisured writer, the scholar, and the stylist." The leisured writer would, I think, be very convenienced by an entry such as this:

writing tool, stylus, style; pencil, lead pencil, mechanical pencil, crayon, chalk; pen (*pen points, when new, will work better if moistened with saliva*)

The next two listings would be convenient for the stylist—specifically, the hair stylist and the song stylist:

hair, filament, down, pubescence, fimbria, fringe, villus, wool, fur, coat, mat, thatch, mop, shock, tangle, shag, mane, pompadour (*with memories of Mme. Pompadour in the black months of the old regime*)

vocalist, singer, melodist, warbler, songbird; songster, songstress, chantress, soprano, mezzo-soprano, contralto; tenor, baritone, bass (*Yma Sumac sings as low as Nelson Eddy and as high as almost anyone*)

As for the scholar, there is no doubt what *that* entry would be, if the Thesaurus were revised along Dr. Mawson's lines:

scholar, learned man . . . classicist, Latinist, Hellenist, Graecist, Hebraist, Sanskritist; Sinologist, Sinologue; linguist, glossolalist; philosopher, philomath, scientist; etymologist, philologist, lexicographer (*dare we include him among the scholars?*)

An almost invaluable aid to the writer is H. W. Fowler's *A Dictionary of Modern Usage.* To Clifton Fadiman, critic, "Information Please" arbiter, and editor of the popular omnibus *Reading I've Liked,* Fowler's book is, however, more than a guide to precision or correctness. It is a "brain-side" book to which one can refer for "spiritual sustenance."

CLIFTON FADIMAN

Commentary on "A Dictionary of Modern English Usage" by H. W. Fowler*

People who try to use the language with respect will do well to keep on hand the fattish, blue-bound volume known as H. W. Fowler's *Dictionary of Modern English Usage*. It should be a brain-side book for every writer, amateur as well as professional, since each of its 742 type-filled pages is a teacher of true humility. I refer to Fowler often, but not necessarily to solve a problem in usage, grammar, or pronunciation. I refer to it for spiritual sustenance. It shows me how bad a writer I am and encourages me to do better.

I am one of that dwindling band that believes the English language, flexible as it is, obeys certain laws and regulations. I do not believe writers are superior to these laws unless, like James Joyce, they have earned the right to that superiority. If a writer is vulgar in mind, sloppy in thought, and crude in manner, his language will betray him; his syntax will find him out. By examining his language with the kind of microscope Fowler supplies, he can spy upon his own defects of character and temperament.

I read, for example, the essays on Genteelisms and Hackneyed Phrases and I realize with a sense of shame that I have been guilty of many of them, not alone in speech but in formal prose. This does not argue that I am a character of black iniquity, but it

* Reprinted from *Reading I've Liked* by Clifton Fadiman, by permission of Simon and Schuster, Inc. © 1941 by Simon and Schuster, Inc.

does point to a tendency of mine to borrow the stale wit and ingenuity of others or to dress up linsey-woolsey thoughts in ostentatious finery. These are small faults of taste and tiny derelictions of morality. They are worth correcting.

Somerset Maugham sums up Fowler thus: "I have read many books on English prose, but have found it hard to profit by them; for the most part they are vague, unduly theoretical, and often scolding. But you cannot say this of Fowler's *Dictionary of Modern English Usage*. It is a valuable work. I do not think anyone writes so well that he cannot learn much from it. It is lively reading. Fowler liked simplicity, straightforwardness and common sense. He had no patience with pretentiousness. He had a sound feeling that idiom was the backbone of a language and he was all for the racy phrase. He was no slavish admirer of logic and was willing enough to give usage right of way through the exact demesnes of grammar."

I must add that Fowler is not only useful but diverting. He is himself, if something of a precisian, a sound writer, witty and ironical when he wishes to be (note, for example, the high comedy in his discourse on the Split Infinitive . . .), and able to make lucid the most subtle and difficult distinctions of usage and shades of linguistic feeling. He is also, on occasion, a vest-pocket essayist of no mean ability, as the little table on Wit, Humor, Irony, etc., indicates. . . .

Word Books

Of all the word books bequeathed to us by the word men whom we have just discussed, the dictionary is, of course, the most valuable. In the following section we shall consider how to choose a dictionary and how to use it effectively.

Mortimer Adler, formerly professor at the University of Columbia and at the University of Chicago, is at present director of the Institute of Philosophical Research. One of the men who popularized the Great Books program, he is also a lecturer and the author of such books as *How to Read a Book* and *How to Think About War and Peace.*

After sampling the astonishing information which a dictionary has to offer and reviewing the history of dictionaries briefly, Adler warns us that we cannot be excused from exercising our own interpretative judgment in reading. The growth of our vocabularies in the important dimension of multiple meanings "will depend upon the character of the books we read." However, Adler continues, the dictionary *can* help to establish the physical aspect of the word, its grammatical role in the sentence, its capacity as a sign, and its conventional aspects, including levels of usage.

Mortimer Adler

How To Read a Dictionary*

The dictionary invites a playful reading. It challenges anyone to sit down with it in an idle moment only to find an hour gone by without being bored. Recently I noticed an advertisement for a dictionary as a wonder book. "Astonished Actually Means Thunderstruck" was the headline, written obviously in the hope that the prospective buyer would be thunderstruck, or wonderstruck, enough to look further. And the rest of the ad listed such tidbits as a "*disaster* literally means 'the stars are against you!' " or "to *tantalize* is to torment with the punishment of Tantalus as told in Greek mythology."

While I do not think astonishment is the dictionary's main mission in life, I cannot resist reporting some of the things I learned accidentally while thumbing its pages, in the course of writing this article. I discovered that the word "solecism" derives from Soli, the name of a Greek colony in Cilicia, whose inhabitants were thought by the Athenians to speak bad Greek; hence, "solecism" was probably the equivalent in Greek slang for a Bostonian's contemptuous reference to "New Yorkese." I learned that "coal" originally meant charred wood. It was then applied to mineral coal when this was first introduced, under such names as "sea-coal" and "pit-coal." Now that mineral coal is the more common variety, we redundantly refer to charred wood as "charcoal."

* Reprinted from "How To Read a Dictionary" by Mortimer Adler in *The Saturday Review of Literature*, December 13, 1941, by permission of *The Saturday Review of Literature*. Copyright 1941 by *The Saturday Review of Literature*.

I was edified by the fact that the drink "Tom and Jerry" derives its name from the two chief characters in Egan's "Life of London" (1821), that in England a low beer joint is called a "Tom and Jerry Shop," and that indulgence in riotous behavior is called "to tom and jerry." I had always thought that a forlorn hope was really a hope on the verge of turning into despair, but it seems that it isn't a hope at all. "Hope" here is a misspelling of the Dutch word "hoop" meaning heap. A forlorn hope is a storming party, a band of heroes who are willing to end up in a heap for their country's cause. And most shocking of all was the discovery that one theory about the origin of the magician's "hocus-pocus" accounts for it as a corruption of "hoc est corpus"—the sacred words accompanying the sacrament of the Eucharist. This, together with the reversal in meaning of "dunce"— from the proper name of Duns Scotus, the subtlest doctor of the Church, to naming a numbskull—provides a two word commentary on the transition from the Middle Ages to modern times.

The staid modern dictionary is full of such wit even when it doesn't try to be funny, as Dr. Johnson did when he defined "oats" as "a grain which in England is generally given to horses, but in Scotland supports the people." Look up "Welsh rabbit," for example, or "scotch capon" or "swiss steak," and you will discover gentle jokes about national shortcomings in diet.

I find that what interests me most of all are the shifts in meaning of common words in daily use. From meaning an attendant on horses, "marshall" has come to mean a leader of men; though also originating in the stable, "constable" has gone in the reverse direction from signifying an officer of highest rank to denoting a policeman; "boon" has done an about-face by becoming the gift which answers a petition, having been the prayer which asked for it. "Magistrate" and "minister" have changed places with each other in the ups and downs of words, for in current political usage, "magistrate" usually names a minor official, whereas "minister" refers to a *major* diplomatic or cabinet post. It is often hard to remember that a minister is a *servant* of the people, and harder still to recall the precise point of religious controversy which caused the substitution of "minister" for "priest" as the name for one who served in the performance of sacerdotal functions. And readers of our Constitution should have their attention called to a shift in the word "citizen" from meaning anyone who, by birth or choice, owes allegiance to the state, to the narrower designation of those who are granted the right to vote. Similarly, "commerce" has narrowed in meaning; like "trade," it once meant every dealing in merchandise, but now is distinguished from industry according to the difference between distributing commodities and producing them.

The word "commerce" reminds me of one other sort of incidental inquiry the dictionary lures you into. You discover that "commerce" and "mercenary" have the same root in *"mercis,"* wares, and that leads you to the closely related root *"merces,"* pay or reward, which is embodied in the word "mercy." If you start this game of research, you will find such roots as *"spec"* from *spectare* meaning to look at or see, which generates a family of 246 English words (species, speculate, specimen, specify, spectacle, inspect, respect, aspect, etc.); or "press" from *"primo"* meaning to squeeze, which has an equally large family (impress, repress, pressing, compress, suppress, oppress, depress, express, etc.).

It is almost as hard to stop writing about the dictionary in this way, as to stop reading one when you are in hot pursuit of the mysteries of human speech. But, over and above such fascinations, the dictionary has its sober uses. To make the most of these one has to know how to read the special sort of book a dictionary is. But, before I state the rules, let me see if I can explain why most people today don't use dictionaries in a manner befitting the purpose for which they were originally created.

In its various sizes and editions, the dictionary is an unlisted best-seller on every season's list. To be able to get along without one would be a sign of supreme literacy—of complete competence as a reader and writer. The dictionary exists, of course, because there is no one in that condition. But, if the dictionary is the necessity we all acknowledge, why is it so infrequently used by the man who owns one? And, even when we do consult it, why do most of us misuse the dictionary or use it poorly?

The answer to both questions may be that few of us make efforts at reading or writing anything above the present level of our literary competence. The books—or maybe it is just the newspapers and magazines—we read, and the things we write, don't send us to the dictionary for help. Our vocabularies are quite adequate, because the first rule in most contemporary writing is the taboo against strange words, or familiar words in strange senses.

Of course, there are always people (not excluding college graduates) who have difficulty with spelling or pronouncing even the common words in daily discourse. That, by the way, is the source of the most frequent impulse to go to the dictionary. There is nothing wrong about this. The dictionary is there to render this simple service—in fact, Noah Webster began his career as the compiler of a spelling book which sold in the millions. But my point remains—the dictionary has other and more important uses, and the reason we do not generally avail ourselves of these services is not our superiority, but rather our lack of need as the life of letters is currently lived.

The history of dictionaries, I think, will bear me out on this point. The Greeks did not have a dictionary, even though "lexicon" is the Greek word for it. The had no need for foreign language dictionaries because there was no literature in a foreign language they cared to read. They had no need for a Greek word-book because the small educated class already knew what such a book would contain. This small group of literate men would have been, like the modern French Academy, the makers of the dictionary, the arbiters of good usage. But at a time when so sharp a line separated the learned from the lewd (which, in an obsolete usage, means *unlettered*), there was no occasion for the few men who could make a dictionary to prepare one for the others.

George Santayana's remark about the Greeks—that they were the only unlettered people in European history—has a double significance. The masses were, of course, uneducated, but even the learned few were not educated in the sense that they had to sit at the feet of foreign masters. Education, in that sense, begins with the Romans, who went to school to Greek pedagogues, and became cultivated through contact with Greek culture. It is not surprising, therefore, that the first dictionaries were glossaries of Homeric words. The earliest lexicon which is still extant is such a glossary, prepared by a Greek, Apollonius, in the fifth century of our era, obviously intended to help Romans read the "Iliad" and "Odyssey" of Homer, as well as other Greek literature which employed the Homeric vocabulary. Most of us today need similar glossaries to read Shakespeare well.

There were dictionaries in the Middle Ages—a famous Latin one by the Spaniard, Isidore of Seville, which was really a philosophical work, a sort of encyclopedia of wordly knowledge accomplished by discussions of the most important technical terms occurring in learned discourse. There were foreign-language dictionaries in the Renaissance (both Latin and Greek) made necessary by the fact that the *humane letters* which dominated the education of the period were from the ancient languages. Even when the vulgar tongues—English, French, or Italian —gradually displaced Latin as the language of learning, the pursuit of learning was still the privilege of the few. Under such circumstances, dictionaries were intended for a limited audience, mainly as an aid to reading the most worthy literature. In attempting to compile a standard dictionary, Dr. Johnson derived his norms from the usage of the best writers, on the theory that this would furnish a guide to others who tried to read them, or who tried to write well.

We see, then, that from the beginning the educational motive dominated the making of dictionaries, though, as in the case of Dr. Johnson, and the work of the French and Italian Academies, there was also an interest in preserving the purity and order of the language. As against the latter interest, the Oxford English Dictionary, begun in 1857, was a new departure, in that it did not try to dictate the best usage, but rather to present an accurate historical record of every type of usage—the worst as well as the best, taken from popular as well as stylish writing. But this conflict between the mission of the lexicographer as self-appointed arbiter and his function as historian can be regarded as a side-issue, for the dictionary, however constructed, is primarily an educational instrument. And the problem is whether that instrument is currently well used.

Our own Noah Webster is in a sense the hero of the story. Alarmed by the state into which learning had fallen after the Revolutionary War, Webster sought to make a one-volume dictionary which would serve in the self-education of the semi-literate masses. He was concerned with the masses, not the elite, and with self-education, at a time when this country had not yet become democratic enough to regard the public education of all its children as a primary obligation of the state. The Webster dictionary was probably one of the first self-help books to become a popular best-seller. And the paradox is that now, with public education widely established in this country, with "literacy" as universal as suffrage, the self-help potentialities of a dictionary are seldom realized by the millions who own one. I am not thinking merely of children from progressive schools who cannot use a dictionary because they do not know the alphabet. I am thinking of all the products of contemporary education who, not being taught or inspired to read the great and difficult books, have little use for the dictionary. *How much better educated was the self-read man whom Webster helped!*

This brief history of dictionaries is relevant to the rules for reading and using them well. One of the first rules as to how to read a book is to know what sort of book it is. That means knowing what the author's intention was and what sort of thing you can expect to find in his work. If you look upon a dictionary merely as a spelling book or a guide to pronunciation, you will use it accordingly. If you realize that it contains a wealth of historical information, crystallized in the growth of language, you will pay attention, not merely to the variety of meanings which are listed under each word, but to their order.

And above all if you are interested in advancing your own education, you will use a dictionary according to its primary intention—as a help in reading books that might otherwise be too difficult because their vocabulary includes technical words, archaic words, literary allusions, or even familiar words used in now obsolete senses. The number of words in a man's vocabulary is as definite as the number of dollars he has in the bank; equally definite is the number of senses in which a man is able to use any given word. But there is this difference: a man cannot draw upon the public treasury when his bank-balance is overdrawn, but we can all draw upon the dictionary to get the coin we need to carry on the transaction of reading anything we want to read.

Let me be sure that I am not misunderstood. I am not saying that a dictionary is all you need in order to move anywhere in the realms of literature. There are many problems to be solved, in reading a book well, other than those arising from the author's vocabulary. And even with respect to vocabulary, the dictionary's primary service is on those occasions when you are confronted with a technical word or with a word that is wholly new to you—such as "costard" (an apple), or "hoatzin" (a South American bird), or "rabato" (a kind of flaring collar). More frequently the problem of interpretation arises because a relatively familiar word seems to be used in a strange sense. Here the dictionary will help, but it will not solve the problem. The dictionary may suggest the variety of senses in which the troublesome word can be used, but it can never determine how the author you are reading used it. That you must decide by wrestling with the context. More often than not, especially with distinguished writers, the word may be given a special, an almost unique, shade of meaning. The growth of your own vocabulary, in the important dimension of multiple meanings as well as in mere quantity of words, will depend, first of all, upon the character of the books you read, and secondly, upon the use you make of the dictionary as a guide. You will misuse it—you will stultify rather than enlighten yourself—as you substitute the dictionary for the exercise of your own interpretative judgment in reading.

This suggests several other rules as to how *not* to read a dictionary. There is no more irritating fellow than the man who tries to settle an argument about communism, or justice, or liberty, by quoting from Webster. Webster and all his fellow lexicographers may be respected as authorities on word-usage, but they are not the ultimate founts of wisdom. They are no Supreme Court to which we can appeal for a decision of those fundamental controversies which, despite the warnings of semanticists, get us involved with abstract words. It is well to remember that the dictionary's authority can, for obvious reasons, be surer in the field of concrete words, and even in the field of the abstract technical words of science, than it ever can be with respect to philosophical words. Yet these words are indispensable if we are going to talk, read, or write about the things that matter most.

Another negative rule is: Don't swallow the dictionary. Don't try to get word-rich quick, by memorizing a lot of fancy words whose meanings are unconnected with any actual experience. Merely verbal knowledge is almost worse than no knowledge at all. If learning consisted in nothing but knowing the meanings of words, we could abolish all our courses of study, and substitute the dictionary for every other sort of book. But no one except a pedant or a fool would regard it as profitable or wise to read the dictionary from cover to cover.

In short, don't forget that the dictionary is a book about words, not about things. It can tell you how men have used words, but it does not define the nature of the things the words name. A Scandinavian university undertook a "linguistic experiment" to prove that human arguments always reduce to verbal differences. Seven lawyers were given seven dictionary definitions of truth and asked to defend them. They soon forgot to stick to the "verbal meanings" they had been assigned, and became vehemently involved in defending or opposing certain fundamental views about the nature of truth. The experiment showed that discussions may start about the meanings of words, but that, when interest in the problem is aroused, they seldom end there. Men pass from words to things, from names to natures. The dictionary can start an argument, but only thought or research can end it.

If we remember that a dictionary is a book about words, we can derive from that fact all the rules for reading a dictionary intelligently. Words can be looked at in four ways.

(1) *Words are physical things*—writable marks and speakable sounds. There must, therefore, be uniform ways of spelling and pronouncing them, though the uniformity is often spoiled by variations.

(2) *Words are parts of speech.* Each single word plays a grammatical role in the more complicated structure of a phrase or a sentence. According to the part it plays, we classify it as a certain part of speech —noun or verb, adjective or adverb, article or preposition. The same word can vary in different usages, shifting from one part of speech to another, as when we say "Man the boat" or "Take the jump." Another sort of grammatical variation in words arises from their inflection, but in a relatively uninflected language like English, we need pay attention only to the conjugation of the verb (infinitive, participle, past tense, etc.), the number of the noun (singular and plural), and the degree of the adjective (especially the comparative and superlative).

(3) *Words are signs.* They have meanings, not one but many. These meanings are related in various ways. Sometimes they shade from one into another; sometimes one word will have two or more sets of totally unrelated meanings. Through their meanings words are related to one another—as synonyms sharing in the same meaning even though they differ in its

shading; or as antonyms through opposition or contrast of meanings. Furthermore, it is in their capacity as signs that we distinguish words as proper or common names (according as they mean just one thing or many which are alike in some respect); and as concrete or abstract names (according as they point to some thing which we can sense, or refer to some aspect of things which we can understand by thought but not observe through our senses).

Finally, (4) *words are conventional.* They mean or signify natural things, but they themselves are not natural. They are man-made signs. That is why every word has a history, just as everything else man makes has a time and place of origin, and a cultural career, in which it goes through certain transformations. The history of words is given by their etymological derivation from original word-roots, prefixes, and suffixes; it includes the account of their physical change, both in spelling and pronunciation; it tells of their shifting meanings, and which among them are archaic and obsolete, which are current and regular, which are idiomatic, colloquial, or slang.

A good dictionary will answer all your questions about words under these four heads. The art of reading a dictionary (as any other book) consists in knowing what questions to ask about words and how to find the answers. I have suggested the questions. The dictionary itself tells you how to find the answers. In this respect, it is a perfect self-help book, because it tells you what to pay attention to and how to interpret the various abbreviations and symbols it uses in giving you the four varieties of information about words. Anyone who fails to consult the explanatory notes and the list of abbreviations at the beginning of a dictionary can blame only himself for not being able to read the dictionary well. Unfortunately, many people fail here as in the case of other books, because they insist upon neglecting the prefatory matter—as if the author were just amusing himself by including it.

I think these suggestions about how to read, and how not to misuse, a dictionary are easy to follow. But like all other rules they will be followed well only by the man who is rightly motivated in the first place. And, in the last place, they will be wisely applied only by the man who remembers that we are both *free* and *bound* in all our dealings with language, whether as writers or readers.

"When I use a word," Humpty-Dumpty said in a rather scornful tone, "it means just what I choose it to mean—neither more nor less."

"The question is," said Alice, "whether you can make words mean so many different things."

"The question is," said Humpty-Dumpty, "which is to be master—that's all!"

The always interesting and frequently diverting fields of slang, colloquialisms, vulgarisms, jargon, codes, and other unconventional forms of language have engaged in large manner the attention of Eric Partridge, one of the most prolific of modern philologists. Whether his immediate study is Shakespeare's bawdy terms or sea slang of the twentieth century, Partridge is, in the judgment of Edmund Wilson,[1] a dictionary maker "unrivalled in his liveliness and terseness." Among Partridge's works are *A Dictionary of Slang and Unconventional English From the Fifteenth Century to the Present Day;*

[1] In "Eric Partridge, the Word King," *The New Yorker*, August 4, 1951, Edmund Wilson, well-known critic, evaluates a few of Mr. Partridge's studies in the field of off-beat, irregular language.

Dictionary of the Underworld, British and American;
Dictionary of Clichés; and *Shakespeare's Bawdy.*

One of the conventional aspects of words referred to
by Adler is levels of usage. After a quick look at the
purists' battle to defend Standard English from usage
which they consider inferior, Eric Partridge explains
what these levels of usage are.

ERIC PARTRIDGE
Slang and Standard English*

For over a century, there have been protests against
the use of slang and controversies on the relation of
slang to the literary language or, as it is now usually
called, Standard English. Purists have risen in their
wrath and conservatives in their dignity to defend the
Bastille of linguistic purity against the revolutionary
rabble. The very vehemence of the attack and the
very sturdiness of the defence have ensured that only
the fittest survive to gain entrance into the citadel,
there establish themselves, and then become conservatives and purists in their turn.

Some of the contestants, however, are uncertain
what they are fighting for—and even what they are
fighting about. They have no very clear ideas as to
what constitutes Standard English, and only the
haziest ideas of what slang is. Even in many esteemed
dictionaries the definitions are unsatisfactory. For instance, in a certain dictionary of acknowledged merit
the definition of slang is: 'Expressions in common
colloquial'—i.e., spoken—'use but not regarded as
Standard English.' Now, that does not go far enough;

* Reprinted from *Here, There and Everywhere* by Eric Partridge,
by permission of Hamish Hamilton, Ltd. Copyright 1950 by Hamish Hamilton, Ltd.

and even in so far as it commits itself it is misleading.

To make himself clear, the quickest and easiest way is for the present writer to be at first arbitrary or even autocratic, and then explanatory.

In every civilized language, there is a hierarchy. That hierarchy consists, in English, of the following ranks, in ascending order of dignity and respectability:—

Cant;

slang;

vulgarisms (in both senses);

colloquialisms;

Standard English, with its three ascending varieties:—

Familiar English;

ordinary Standard English;

literary English

(Dialect stands rather to one side; it cannot fairly be placed in the hierarchy at all, for it is primitive and regional. Nevertheless, it forms one of the sources from which Standard English is recruited.)

Cant, more generally know as 'the language of the underworld,' is the special vocabulary—rather is it a set of interconnected vocabularies—of criminals and tramps and beggars, of their hangers-on and associates, and of racketeers.

Slang may be replenished, indeed it often is replenished, by recruits from the underworld, but usually it stands self-dependent and self-sufficient, until it dies of inanition or weariness or a change in fashion or, on the other hand, so strongly survives that it is adopted and becomes a colloquialism and is subject to the conditions affecting and governing colloquialisms.

Colloquialisms stand midway between slang and

Standard English: they are felt to be more respectable, more permanent than slang, but less respectable, less dignified than Standard English. They are called colloquialisms because they are general and fitting enough in conversation but hardly fitting in serious writings, speeches, sermons. They are used by a larger proportion of the population than is slang.

Standard English is such English as is held to be proper and respectable, fitting and dignified, in all conditions; moreover and especially it consists of all such language as is both adequate and seemly on all serious occasions and in communication with foreigners. The best, the predominant variety of Standard English is that which is neither homely (Familiar English) nor elevated (Literary English). Familiar English is that which is suitable and natural in the ordinary commerce of speech and writing; Literary English is that which is used upon solemn or very important occasions, in sustained and deliberate eloquence, in the most philosophical or aesthetic writings or wherever also the writer may feel that, to do justice to the theme, he must employ only the finest language. Obviously the borderlines between Familiar English, ordinary Standard English, and Literary English are often ill-defined; and the distinctions between these three varieties are much less important than the differences between cant and slang, between slang and colloquialisms, and between colloquialisms and Standard English.

But what of vulgarisms?

Vulgarisms are of two kinds: illiteracies and low language. Illiteracies are, as their name indicates, words and phrases used only by the illiterate: that is, they are words and phrases used incorrectly. Low language, again obviously, consists of expressions avoided by the polite and the decent, at least in polite or decent company. These expressions are not illiterate, they may even be good English—but such good English as, by the association of ideas and by social habit, has come to be avoided in polite company. For instance, *pluck* was once both slang and a vulgarism; at first, the synonymous *guts* was likewise both slang and a vulgarism. In the hierarchy, vulgarisms may be adjudged co-equal with slang or, at lowest, lying somewhere between cant and slang.

But these generalities remain vague and highhanded unless examples are adduced. Without examples, they are as nothing; more, they are nothing. When Dickens speaks of *cracking a rib* (breaking into a building in order to steal certain contents) he is using cant; it is, by the way, obsolete cant. When a 20th Century novelist or journalist uses the phrase *wide boys*, he also is using cant. If we allude to someone as *a queer fish* or *a rum fellow* we are using slang, for either expression is understood by almost everyone—it is not confined to the underworld, is in fact no longer used by the underworld. When an airman refers to himself as a *penguin*, he is resorting to the specialized slang of the Air Force; all he means is that he is a member of the ground staff and therefore does not fly; a New Zealand airman would call himself a *kiwi*. Neither a penguin nor a kiwi is a flying bird. If someone calls you *a good chap* or *a decent fellow*, he is employing a colloquialism; for some years, the latter phrase has been qualifying for, though it has not yet achieved, the status of Familiar English. A *nice* (or *decent*) *man* is Standard English. If I say, 'Come, lass,' I am using Familiar English;

if I address her as 'Dear girl,' I am using ordinary Standard English; and if I say, 'Come, sweet maid,' I am using Literary English. If, however, I allude to the girl as a *dame* or a *Jane*, I am employing slang; if as a *moll*, I am employing cant; if as—but perhaps I had better not particularize the vulgarisms for 'girl' or 'woman.'. . . .

Problems of Conformity

Such word books as those we have just discussed can help us with a variety of language problems. One of the most baffling of such problems is deciding what correct speech is. The following section suggests standards which will help us to choose the proper dialect and to speak an easy, natural English. Another problem dealt with is spelling.

Of the three principal dialects spoken in the United States—Eastern, Southern, and General—which is the "correct" one for us? In the following excerpt from *Basic Voice Training for Speech,* Elise Hahn, Donald E. Hargis, Charles W. Lomas, and Daniel Vandraegen—all members of the Speech Department at the University of California at Los Angeles—answer this pertinent question. They discuss, too, the diacritical markings used by the dictionaries to indicate pronunciation and the more precise phonetic symbols devised by the linguists.

Elise Hahn, Donald E. Hargis, Charles
W. Lomas, and Daniel Vandraegen

Articulation Standards: How to
Select a Standard*

The pattern of English speech varies widely
throughout the world. You are familiar with such
broad variations as British and American speech; you
are probably aware of the existence of three widely
spoken American dialects: Eastern, Southern, and
General. Each of these dialects has marked differences within itself. There are also some dialects, confined to narrow geographical limits, which are not
readily classifiable into any regional division. The
latter, however, are not spoken by educated people,
who tend to adopt some form of one of the three
main patterns.

Dialects differ from one another primarily in pro-
nunication, but variations in melody pattern, rhythm,
and colloquial vocabulary also exist. Among the British dialects you probably have heard are the familiar
"standard British," spoken by British statesmen and
other public figures, the Cockney, Lancashire, Scottish, and Irish dialects. In the United States, if you
have traveled in the South, you will recognize that
differences exist between the pronunciation patterns
of Richmond, Virginia, and those of Charleston,
South Carolina, or Dallas, Texas, although all three
are recognizably Southern. The speech of the educated
New Yorker is unlike that of the Bostonian, and
neither is quite like that of the resident of the Maine

* By permission from *Basic Voice Training for Speech*, by Hahn,
Lomas, Hargis, and Vandraegen. Copyright, 1952, by McGraw Hill
Book Company, Inc.

coast. Less marked but nevertheless perceptible differences exist among speech patterns of Indiana, Iowa, and Nebraska. In cosmopolitan areas like New York City or Los Angeles, where those born elsewhere frequently outnumber the natives, the dialects of all areas, including those derived from the influence of foreign languages, are mingled in indescribable confusion.

"If this is the case," you say, "how may I know what is the 'correct' articulation of the words I use?". . .

For most of the speaking you do, your standard should be that employed by the educated people of the broad dialect region in which you live. For a large majority of Americans, this dialect is the one we have called General American, some form of which is spoken throughout the United States, except in portions of New England and elsewhere along the Atlantic seaboard, and in the South. Southerners and Easterners, of course, should retain the characteristic features of their own dialects. This does not mean accepting all the local peculiarities of the speech in your immediate area. Franklin Roosevelt's speech, for example, was distinctly Eastern, but was largely free from localisms. Alfred E. Smith's speech, on the other hand, was so highly localized as to be a matter of amusement and even resentment to the radio audience outside New York City. Speech which is acceptable to educated people in any of the three major dialect areas will not be displeasing to discriminating hearers in either of the other regions. You should therefore concentrate on learning clear articulation of speech within your own regional dialect. At the same time, you should learn the main differences between the way you speak and the speech used elsewhere in the English-speaking world. . . .

The pronunciations given in carefully edited dictionaries are, for the most part, those of formal speech. Statesmen, leading public speakers, actors, radio personalities, chairmen of university English departments, and other public figures are consulted. Their pronunciation of words is analyzed by the editors of the dictionary. Where conflicts occur, the most commonly used pronunciations are selected and recorded in the dictionary as "standard." The dictionary is therefore an excellent guide to the pronunciation of words in isolation as used by the best educated men in formal speech. However, it does not reflect many of the changes in the articulation pattern which occur in the less formal situations, nor can it show adequately the changes in the pattern induced by the proximity of other words or by the position of words in a sentence. If you rely merely on the list of symbols often given at the bottom of each page, the dictionary does not discriminate between dialects in different parts of the United States, although these differences are dealt with in the more detailed guides to pronunciation given in good dictionaries. One recent dictionary, the sixth edition of Webster's Collegiate Dictionary, eliminates the symbols from the bottom of the page to compel the reader to examine the guide in the introduction. . . .

When written languages were first developed, the symbols used were supposed to represent sounds, and to some extent this original function of the alphabet has persisted. In some languages, alphabetical symbols come much closer to representing sounds than in English. The difficulty in English spelling arises from two chief sources: (1) the diverse origin of English words; (2) the failure of spelling reform to keep pace with changes in pronunciation. Modern English words are derived from virtually every language root, but the most common ones are Anglo-Saxon (of Germanic origin), Norman French, Latin, and Greek. The English spelling of words is generally a direct derivation from the original root, each of which has a somewhat different system of sound symbols. These divergencies have never been reconciled, nor has any systematic spelling reform ever been undertaken to bring them all into a common system. . . .

Dictionary editors have attempted to solve the problem of representing sounds by respelling words and supplementing the alphabetical symbols with a system of dots and lines known as *diacritical markings*. This is a decided improvement over English spelling as a manner of representing sounds, and for the pronunciation of words in isolation, it is perhaps accurate enough for most uses. Diacritical systems, however, although they are similar, are not uniform. In order to interpret a dictionary pronunciation accurately, you must consult the guide to pronunciation for that particular dictionary. Webster's Collegiate Dictionary, for example, lists sixty-six symbols in the key to pronunciation, whereas the American College Dictionary lists only forty-eight, some of which are quite different from Webster's symbols.

In addition to this, diacritical markings do not distinguish among different dialects, in many cases. The symbol à as it is used in the Webster dictionaries is dependent on your pronunciation of the word *ask*. However, the pronunciation of this word varies from one part of the country to another—from the A in *father*, to the A in *bat*. The symbol à is thus accurate enough to give you the pronunciation of other words in your own dialect, but it is not exact enough to represent the sounds of speech as you hear others produce them. Since the symbol represents a broad range of usage, it cannot represent an exact sound. Precisely the same difficulty is encountered in words marked with the symbol ŏ, since varying interpretations render the symbol ambiguous.

In order to transcribe and study spoken language, scholars have developed phonetic symbols for each sound. Often the alphabet letter can be used to represent a sound. For such sound units, however, as CH, TH, and NG, where there is no single letter to indicate the sounds, or for vowels where the letter stands for a variety of sounds, special symbols had to be created.

By means of such symbols, a written record can be made, for example, of the different ways in which men from the various regions in this country or from foreign countries may say the same word or phrase. Also, by means of phonetics, the listener can record the changes which take place in sounds when they occur together and affect each other's production or when they are stressed or unstressed in the flow of speech.

The use of phonetics, then, permits accuracy in the transcription of speech. . . .

J. B. Priestley, English essayist, novelist, and playwright, is the author of such works as *The Good Companions, Essayists Past and Present, Midnight on the Desert*, and *Arts Under Socialism*. Mr. Priestley tells us that he himself would never choose the following article to reprint; but it is important to us because, among other reasons, Mr. Priestley assures us here that Great Britain also takes substantially the position just stated in "How to Select a Standard" concerning the choice of the "right" accent. He cites the varieties of speech heard in the House of Commons to prove his contention that there is no such thing as standardization.

J. B. PRIESTLEY

The Right Accent*

If, as we are told, some candidates for commissions in the Royal Navy have recently been rejected because they do not speak with the right accent, then there must be some very foolish fellows holding high rank in the Navy. They should think again, at least find a better excuse for turning down young men they did not like. This accent business simply will not do.

Let us admit at once that there is a difference between educated and uneducated speech, and that the Sea Lords are entitled to demand that their officers should speak like educated men. Nobody holding a responsible position should indulge in really slovenly speech, with most consonants missing, like that of lads who hang about street corners. But accent is something quite different. In Britain you cannot insist that a man shall use "the right accent." There is no such thing.

What is called "the B.B.C. Accent" is simply standardized South-country English. It does not sug-

* Reprinted from "The Right Accent" by J. B. Priestley in the *New York Times Magazine*, May 2, 1954, by permission of the author and of the *New York Times Magazine*.

gest any particular locality. It is a good accent for English radio men when what is aimed at is an impersonal sort of voice, making impersonal announcements, reading the news and so forth; also for actors. But there is no particular reason why a naval officer should use it.

The so-called "Oxford Accent" is quite different. It has nothing to do with the University of Oxford. It is still heard a good deal in pulpits, and also among men who have old-fashioned ideas about social grandeur. It is a rather affected drawl, and has what seem to my ear some murderous vowel sounds, the most frequent being an "ah" sound—so that "Here, Mr. Chairman!" becomes, "Heah, Mister Charman!" And if young naval officers are being encouraged to talk like this, we shall have to put our trust in the R.A.F.

In point of fact, most people here who are not compelled, for professional reasons, to adopt the standardized B.B.C. accent, usually show traces of local accent. And this is certainly true of exceptionally distinguished men, as I have noticed over and over again. Take my own profession. Great writers can hardly be dismissed as uneducated and uncultured speakers, yet most of them I have known have had very definite local accents. Thus, Shaw had a pronounced Dublin brogue, H. G. Wells a high Cockney twang, Barrie a marked Scots accent, and Arnold Bennett clearly showed his upbringing in the North Midlands. And in clubs and other places where men high in their various professions can be overheard talking eagerly, I have listened with interest and pleasure to the variety of their accents, hearing the map of the British Isles coming to life.

My own Yorkshire accent is plain to all ears, and it

has never occurred to me to change it. In my opinion, it is a very good accent, if only because it gives full weight to all the vowel sounds, which enables it, among other things, to do justice to poetry. I found it a great asset during the war when I had to speak regularly over the radio to all parts of the British Empire and to the United States. My accent might be strange to many of these listeners but they could understand what I said, and probably felt they were being addressed by a man and a brother, and not by a sinister English aristocrat with a monocle. I admit that the monocle voice is still with us, using a variety of "Oxford Accent," but one hears it less and less every year. It belongs essentially to the nineteenth century, when the ruling-class English could afford to sound very fancy indeed, drawling away to prove they had not to earn a living or conciliate their hearers. It is no accent for a man who is desperately trying to increase his export trade.

Old-fashioned snobbery dies hard, however, and I have heard rumors of this accent nonsense playing its part in other Government departments besides the Admiralty. The private tastes and prejudices of senior civil servants come in here. Thus, to some men's ears a broad North-country or Devon accent sounds comic, so that they feel that a man with such an accent might have a difficult time in a responsible position. (The fact that comedians often use such accents is perhaps important here.) However, there is no place in Britain where you can hear a greater variety of accents than the House of Commons. And in this it is truly representative.

The great mistake—and I cannot say if the Admiralty made it or not—is to confuse a sensible local accent with really bad slovenly speech. For the latter I hold no brief whatever. I hear children now, especially in the cities, talking in an appalling fashion, so devoid of sharp consonants and proper vowel sounds that it might be the mumbling of a village idiot. Down, I say, with any candidate who talks like that. If his speech is so faulty, he probably cannot think. He does not propose to take trouble about anything. I would not trust him with a toy yacht, let alone a battleship. So if their Sea Lordships turned down a few youths who talked in this fashion, then I do not blame them.

But if they really believe that good naval officers can only be made out of men who do not keep their vowels open then I cannot cry "Heah, heah!" or give them "Three chars!"

I have heard it suggested—in America—that the "upper class" English accent has been of value in maintaining the British Empire and Commonwealth. The argument runs that all manner of folk in distant places, understanding the English language, will catch in this accent the notes of tradition, pride and authority and so will be suitably impressed. This might have been the case fifty years ago but it is certainly not true now. This is more likely to be a liability than an asset.

It is significant that the Royal Family in their speeches and broadcasts use a considerably modified form of the accent. The public English of George V was magnificently free from all affectations. His children and grandchildren have done their best to follow his example.

In point of fact that famous hawhaw English accent is rapidly vanishing from the world of debate, decision and action. Men who have to talk politics or business with Americans, Canadians, Australians and others soon find such an accent a disadvantage. It is not always easily understood. It sounds patronizing, supercilious or just comic. International conferences, together with the influence of talking pictures and radio, have given that English accent a push westward.

Men of affairs have tended to copy those actors of ours who have spent years in Hollywood and have there gradually modified their original accent. There is, indeed, now an accent that might well be called the Mid-Atlantic.

In a new novel, J. D. Scott makes the same point. He is discussing this move westward in speech—"It is the accent of the future, standard Princeton-Anglo-American, clear, articulate and amiable. It is readily understood by subject races. It doesn't arouse the worst instincts of the lower orders like standard Mayfair-County-and-Peerage."

He might have added, too, that the new accent not only does its job better than the old but that it is also much better English. Its vowel sounds are at once more varied and more honest than the old (though not as good as those I learned from my North-country parents). It does not suggest an inflexible attitude toward the world. It serves well either for negotiation or oratory. I do not want it to take the place of all our local accents—yours as well as mine—but if there is to be some sort of standard English for public life, the theatre, the screen and radio, then the new mid-Atlantic accent seems to me to have the strongest claim.

While I am on this subject I should like somebody

to answer a question. When some American writers want to have some fun with an English accent they make it say "veddy," presumably instead of "very." Now I pride myself on having a good ear but never, listening to every possible type of Englishman, have I ever heard this "veddy." Where does it come from? I find it veddy veddy puzzling.

Morris Bishop explains how to do away with the exasperating problems of rendering dialect in print by using another exasperating linguistic device, the phonetic alphabet.

MORRIS BISHOP

How To Write Sho-Nuf Dialect*

Exasperating indeed are the approximations of writers
    of dialect,
The study of which surely neither you nor I elect;
Nor would any but a greenhorn whose hair is full of
    alfalfa bet
These writers had ever even heard of the International
    Phonetic Alphabet.
Do they mean "onct" to rhyme with "honked" or
    "thou grunt'st"?
The I.P.A. would clarify it as "wʌnst."
Instead of dragging us through "Hit shore peahs lak a
    right tol'able mawnin'"
Give us "hɪt ʃɔr pjɛ·z laķ ə rɑ·t talǝbl mɔ·nɪn."
Or instead of "Och, 'tis gey braw an' bricht the
    morrn,"

* © 1948 The New Yorker Magazine, Inc.

I urge: "ɔç, tɪz gəɪ brɔ ən brɪçt ðə mɔɪ̇n."

And if you plead that phonetic transcription is un-
readable,

Why, the unreadability of all dialect shore is purty
pleadable.

—mɔrɪs bɪʃʌp

**The difference between dialectal pronunciations is
exaggerated to the point of absurdity by Ogden Nash,
singer of all manner of dilemmas, even semantic ones.**

Ogden Nash

This Is My Own, My Native Tongue*

Often I leave my television set to listen to my wireless,

So, often I hear the same song sung by the same singer
many times a day, because at repeating itself the
wireless is tireless.

There is one such song from which at sleepy time I can
hardly bear to part,

A song in which this particular singer, who apparently
has offended a nameless character in an unde-
scribed way, states that he apawlogizes from the
bawttom of his heart.

I am familiar with various accents—I know that in
Indiana you stress the "r" in Carmen,

And that in Georgia if a ladybug's house is on far she
sends for the farmen,

And I have paaked my caah in Cambridge, and elsewhere spoken with those who raise hawgs and

* Reprinted by permission of the author. Originally published in
The New Yorker Magazine. © 1949 and 1951 by Ogden Nash.

worship strange gawds—but here I am, late in
    life's autumn,
Suddenly confronted with somebody's apawlogies and
    bawttom.
I tell you whawt,
Things were different when I was a tawddling tawt.
I may have been an indifferent schawlar,
Lawling around in my blue serge suit and doodling on
    my Eton cawllar;
In fact, I didn't even pick up much knawledge
In a year at cawllege;
I guess that of normal intelligence I had only about
    two thirds,
But, by gum, I was taught, or, by gum, was I tot, to
    pronounce my words.
And now they've gawt me wondering:
Was it the dawn or the don that from China cross the
    bay came up thundering?
As a tot, was I tawddling or was I toddling?
When I doodled, was I dawdling or was I dodling?
I have forgawtten oll I ever knew of English, I find
    my position as an articulate mammal bewildering
    and awesome.
Would God I were a tender apple blawssom.

In addition to pronouncing our words correctly—the
problem previously discussed in "How to Select a Standard"—we "Murcans" must mind our enunciation, too,
as we are reminded in the following article by John
Davenport, vice-president of the Industrial Engineering
Corporation of Louisville. Davenport's "Slurvian" grew
out of a word game which he had invented.

JOHN DAVENPORT

Slurvian Self-Taught*

Listening to a well-known Hollywood commentator some time back, I heard her say that she had just returned from a Yerpeen trip, and had had a lovely time nittly. I at once recognized her as an accomplished Slurvian linguist and, being a student of Slurvian, readily understood that she had just returned from a European trip, and while there (in Yerp) had had a lovely time in Italy.

Slurvian is coming into common use in the United States, but I am, so far as I know, the only scholar to have made a start toward recording it. There is no official written Slurvian language, but it is possible, by means of phonetic spelling, for me to offer a brief course of instruction in it. In a short time, the student can learn enough to add immeasurably to his understanding and enjoyment wherever he travels in the country.

I first heard pure Slurvian fluently spoken by a co-worker of mine who told me that his closest friend was a man named Hard (Howard). Hard was once in an automobile accident, his car, unfortunately, cliding with another, causing Hard's wife Dorthy, who was with him, to claps. Dorthy didn't have much stamina but was a sweet woman—sweet as surp.

I soon discovered I had an ear for Slurvian, and since I began to recognize the language, I have encountered many Slurvians. At ballparks, they keep track of hits, runs, and airs. On farms, they plow furs.

* Reprinted by permission of the author. Originally published in *The New Yorker Magazine*. © 1949 by The New Yorker Magazine, Inc.

In florist shops, they buy flars. When hard up, they bar money from banks, and spend it for everything from fewl for the furnace to grum crackers for the children.

When Slurvians travel abroad, they go to visit farn (or forn) countries to see what the farners do that's different from the way we Murcans do things. While in farn countries, they refer to themselves as Murcan tersts, and usually say they will be mighty glad to get back to Murca. A Slurvian I once met on a train told me he had just returned from a visit to Mexico. He deplored the lack of automobiles down there, and said that the natives ride around on little burrs.

A linguistic authority of my acquaintance, much interested in my work in Slurvian, has suggested to me the possiblity that the language may be related to, or a variation of, the one still spoken in England of which such a contraction as "Chumley," for "Cholmondeley," is a familiar example. However, I think the evidence insufficient for drawing such a conclusion. Surnames cannot he considered subject to the ordinary rules of pronunciation. In fact, the only one I have positively identified in Slurvian is Faggot, the name of the American admiral who won the Battle of Mobile Bay.

The name Faggot brings me to a discussion of what I designate as "pure" Slurvian. This includes those Slurvian words that, when spelled exactly as pronounced, also make good English words (such as "Faggot," "burr," and "claps"). The day I can add to the lexicon such a word, hitherto unrecorded, is a happy day for me. Here are some examples of pure Slurvian, alphabetically listed:

bean, *n.* A living creature, as in *human bean.*

cactus, *n. pl.* The people in a play or story.

course, *n.* A group of singers.

fiscal, *adj.* Pertaining to the body, as opposed to the spurt.

form, n. Gathering place of the ancient Romans.

gnome, *n.* Contraction for *no, Ma'am. Colloq.*

line, *n.* The king of beasts.

lore, *n.* The more desirable of the two berths in a Pullman section.

myrrh, *n.* A looking glass.

par, *n.* An attribute of strength, as in *the par and the glory.*

plight, *adj.* Courteous.

sears, *adj.* Grave, intent.

sport, *v.t.* To hold up, to bear the weight of.

wreckers, *n. pl.* Discs on which music is recorded for phonographs.

I am presently engaged in compiling a dictionary of Slurvian words, which I hope will prove to be the definitive work on the subject. The help of any interested students is welcomed, but I must caution such students to be certain the words are genuine Slurvian, and not merely regional speech, such as that of Alabama, Texas, or New England.

Let me close with a final example, to make my meaning clear. Wherever you may be in the United States, if you hear the word "tare," the speaker probably is not referring to a Biblical weed growing in the wheat. More likely, he is describing the sensation of extreme fear experienced by a movie fan watching Borse Karloff in a harr picture.

Pronunciation difficulties are ridiculed in the following verse by Ilo Orleans, who shows that a perfectionist may easily drive himself mad.

Ilo Orleans

V-A-N G-O-G-H
(*Pronounced* Van Gogh)*

Today his paintings are the vogue;
And all the world salutes Van Gogh.
But there are folks, not bright enough
Correctly to pronounce Van Gogh.
Perplexed, bewildered, all agog,
They venture, haltingly, Van Gogh.
Or hem and haw or grunt or cough,
And hastily suggest Van Gogh.
Or cough or grunt or hew or haw,
And then, inspired, blurt out Van Gogh.
While others, with deep furrowed brow,
Determine that he is Van Gogh.
And some there are, content and smug,
Who are convinced he is Van Gogh.
And do not smile and think it gauche
If someone states he is Van Gogh.
Or if a haugty lass says, "Bosh!
The artist's name is clear, Van Gogh."
Or Herr von Schnauzer cries out, "Och!
Der painter's namen iss Van Gogh."
But since I also do not know,
I nonchalantly say *Van Gogh*.

* By permission of the author. From *Word Study*, copyright, 1941, by G. & C. Merriam Co.

Another problem, serious this time, to which there is no solution is that of spelling. The following article offers no hope of eliminating the difficulty. It does, however, point out its complexity and convinces us of the necessity of putting up with the situation pretty much as it is.

FALK JOHNSON

Should Spelling Be Streamlined?*

If English-speaking peoples will streamline their spelling, reshaping it to fit pronunciation, they will soon save enough money to pay the entire cost of World War II. George Bernard Shaw repeatedly states this opinion in letters to the London *Times*, and so do many other contributors to the *Times*.

On this side of the Atlantic, too, the demand for reform in spelling is strong. For example, in the *Journal of the National Education Association*, Dr. Frank C. Laubach, who has developed at Columbia University a new system know as "Basic Spelling," declared last year: "I have asked several hundred audiences how many favor reformed spelling and three fourths of them have raised their hands for it. Often it was unanimous."

Such demands for reform indicate that something is seriously wrong with spelling, and even the opponents of reform admit that the present system is far from perfect. What are its defects? What causes them? What are their consequences in the everyday

* Reprinted from "Should Spelling Be Streamlined?" by Falk Johnson in *The American Mercury*, September, 1948, by permission of the author and of *The American Mercury*.

use of the language? And can anything be done to eliminate them?

According to the reformers, the chief defect is that spelling is not based upon pronunciation, that the symbols of the language do not fit the sounds of the language. Perhaps they never fitted. Certainly they have not fitted since the time, about two thousand years ago, when the Romans gave their alphabet to our linguistic forefathers, for this alphabet does not provide a letter for every sound.

Commenting upon this fact, Shaw says: "Our attempts to make a foreign alphabet of 26 letters do the work of 42 are pitiable. We write the same vowel twice to give it a different sound . . . we also double the final consonant . . . or make two consonants represent simple sounds for which the Latin alphabet does not provide."

As a result of these discrepancies between alphabet and pronunciation, most letters represent several sounds. The Merriam-Webster dictionary, for example, lists eight different pronunciations for the letter *a* and illustrates them by the following words: *ale*, *chaotic*, *care*, *add*, *account*, *arm*, *ask*, and *sofa*. (The *a* in *ale* is accented, that in *chaotic* unaccented.)

Since individual letters may thus represent several different sounds, the relationship between symbol and sound is extremely variable. These relationships may be described as "variable sounds."

But there are also "variable symbols"—several different letters which represent a single sound. For instance, both *e* and *ee* in *melee* have the same sound as *a* in *ale*.

Some of these variable symbols can be traced to the invasion of England, about nine hundred years ago, by William the Conqueror. His followers introduced into the language thousands of words which had French spellings for English sounds. *Ale*, for example, has an "English" spelling for this *a* sound, and *melee* has two "French" spellings for it.

Other variable symbols are the result of a widespread and evolutionary change in pronunciation. This change, called the Great Vowel Shift, is illustrated by the fact that the *Eng* in the word English was once pronounced and spelled *Ang* (Angle); then it was pronounced and spelled *Eng* (English); and now, though it is still spelled *Eng*, it is pronounced *ing*. Thus the letters *e*, *i*, and certain other vowels often represent the same sound.

Variable symbols, however, are made even more variable and bewildering by the inclusion of silent letters. The sound of *a* in *ale*, for example, is represented in *day*, not only by an *a*, but also by a silent *y*.

Many of the letters now silent in the language were pronounced about five hundred years ago, when Caxton introduced printing into England and quite naturally included them in his printed words. Since then, however, they have disappeared from the spoken language but have persisted, imbedded like fossils, in the written language. For instance, the *l* in *would* was pronounced in Caxton's day; now, though unpronounced, it still remains in the spelling.

Some silent letters, however, were never pronounced. The *h* in *ghost* is an example. Knowing that there was an *h* in the Dutch word for *ghost*, the typesetters Caxton brought from Holland assumed that there was an *h* in the English word, too; and they inserted it there. It has been there ever since. In fact, it has spread to other words. Two hundred years ago when Dr. Samuel Johnson published his famous dictionary—for a long time the chief authority in spelling —he put the *h* in *ghastly* and *aghast*, presumably to make them more ghostly.

Today the silent letters are everywhere. Almost every letter is, at some time or another, silent. The following illustrations involve fifteen of the first sixteen letters of the alphabet: an *a* in *head*, *b* in *lamb*, *c* in *indict*, *d* in *handsome*, *e* in *love*, *f* in *off*, *g* in *gnaw*, *h* in *shepherd*, *i* in *weird*, *k* in *knee*, *l* in *salmon*, *m* in *mnemonics*, *n* in *condemn*, *o* in *too*, and *p* in *psychology*.

Some words, like *psychology*, have two silent letters; some, like *though*, three; and some like *thoroughfare*, four. (Knickknack, an incredible word, which includes a silent double k, has the same letter silent four times.) In all, English contains hundreds of thousands of silent letters. Of the 604,000 words in the Merriam-Webster unabridged dictionary, over 400,000 have at least one silent letter; and many, of course, have more than one.

Only after these hundreds of thousands of silent letters have been added to the variable symbols which (like the *a* and *e* in *ale* and *melee*) involve no silent letters at all, can the total number of variable symbols in the language be computed.

So far, it has not been computed, but it is obviously tremendous. For example, a single one of the eight *a* sounds is represented by at least fourteen different symbols: *a* in *ale*, *ae* in *maelstrom*, *ai* in *bait*, *ao* in *gaol* (pronounce *jail*), *au* in *gauge*, *ay* in *day*, *aye* in *aye* (meaning *always*), both *e* and *ee* in *melee*, *ea* in *break*, *eh* in *eh*, *ey* in *prey*, *et* in *beret*, and *eigh* in *weigh*.

There are so many variable symbols that the short word *circus* can be spelled in scores of different ways, all of them closely paralleled by "good" English spellings. A sample is *psoloquoise*. In it, the first *c* of *circus* is pronounced like the *ps* of *psychology;* the *ir* of *circus* like the *olo* of *colonel;* the second *c* of *circus* like the *qu* of *bouquet;* and *us* of *circus* like the *oise* of *tortoise.*

When to all these variable symbols are added the variable sounds (such as those of *a* in *ale, add,* etc.), the enormity of the difference between spelling and pronunciation becomes clear. It has been estimated that eighty per cent (or about a half million) of the words in English are not spelled phonetically. As a result, dictionaries must use one combination of symbols to show the spelling of a word, another to show its pronunciation. It is evident, therefore, that English is not one language, but two—a written and a spoken one.

As a consequence, all English-speaking peoples must learn two languages instead of one. They have no trouble, of couse, with the spoken language. As children, they pick it up naturally and effortlessly, with no formal instruction. They could learn the written language with little trouble, too, if it corresponded systematically to the spoken one. All they would have to do would be to learn the letters; then they could spell immediately any word that they could pronounce.

But, because there is no systematic correspondence between symbol and sound, children are compelled to study spelling for years—all the way through grade school and at least part of the way through high school. Even then it is not mastered, however, and most well-educated adults must have a dictionary nearby when they write. The truth is that no one is infallible in his choice between such variable symbols as *ei* and *ie*, *able* and *ible*; and no one, deprived of a dictionary, can spell all the words in the language. Thus spelling, which should be as easy and effortless as speaking, is a lifetime task—long, costly and unnecessary.

The amount of time and taxes which English-speaking peoples waste in trying to learn to spell cannot be accurately determined, but a former superintendent of schools in New York City has declared that he is "quite confident" that each individual devotes to it the equivalent of from one to two years. Since 260 million individuals know English, it is possible, therefore, that during every generation the equivalent of a quarter or half billion man-years is squandered on spelling.

The loss of time is even greater, however, in the everyday uses of the language than in the learning of it. Most persons spend much more time in using it—reading it, writing it, typing it, linotyping it or printing it—than in learning it.

Waste occurs because these processes use, for example, *though* with six letters, instead of *tho*, with three. The longer form doubles the work of all writers, typists, typesetters and readers. It leads to unnecessary costs, not only for labor, but also for paper, machinery, electricity, transportation, and all other supplies and services needed for the production and "consumption" of the written language.

No estimates are available for the total losses incurred in the uses of the language, but they must be incredibly large. When added to those in learning the language, they may well be as great as Shaw suggested —as great as the total cost of the war itself.

The proponents of spelling reform believe that such losses cannot be ignored. Instead, the system must be changed, its inadequate alphabet enlarged and its variable spellings regularized.

But is it actually possible to change a system of spelling? Is it actually possible to change anything—even if it is unreasonable and wasteful—that is so deeply ingrained in the linguistic habits of a quarter of a billion people living on separate continents? In brief, even if the present system should be changed, can it be changed?

Answers to these questions differ, but the proponents of spelling reform say that the needed changes can be made. As proof, they point out that spelling has changed in every period in which the language has been recorded. For example, the medieval spellings *housbonde, mynde,* and *ygone* have been replaced by the modern *husband, mind,* and *gone.* As recently as the last century Noah Webster, for a while an enthusiastic advocate of reform, was instrumental in throwing the final *k* out of such words as *musick* and *logick.* History proves that changes have been made in the past; why cannot they be made in the future?

The plans for change are, roughly speaking, of two types—those which favor phonetic spelling and those which favor simplified spelling. Proponents of the phonetic system believe that spelling can be efficient only if it corresponds exactly to pronunciation. Consequently they sacrifice everything, including resemblance to current spellings, in order to align symbol with sound.

In this process they replace the present alphabet with a new one. Numerous phonetic alphabets have been devised for this purpose, but the best known of them is the IPA (for International Phonetic Association). It was developed by Paul E. Passy and has often been used in dictionaries, in textbooks dealing with the pronunciation of foreign languages, and in the technical literature of the phoneticians.

Though phonetic spelling has many important technical uses, its chances of superseding the present system are extremely small. It is too revolutionary. For example, if it were adopted, all alphabetized books, indexes, and files would have to be revised according to the new alphabet. All typewriters, linotypes, and other writing machines would have to be re-designed, and their users would have to be re-trained. All adults would have to be re-trained to read the "new" publications; and children would have to be "double-trained" —that is, they would have to be taught both the new and the old methods of reading.

It is no wonder, therefore, that American publications often ridicule proposals for phonetic spelling. *Time* magazine considered Shaw's proposal as a "notion"; and *Newsweek* dismissed it in a brief, disparaging article entitled "Pshaw on Pspelling."

Most reformers, however, do not recommend anything so drastic as phonetic spelling. They do not believe that the present system should be replaced by a new one or that the present alphabet should be tampered with. Rather, they want to keep—and gradually to simplify—the present system. For example, they would remove only one *k* at a time from *knock*. By persisting in such gradual changes, they believe that they can eventually rid the language of its wasteful spelling and evolve a new system closely resembling pronunciation.

The degree of success which such a policy of moderation can have is illustrated by the experience of the Simplified Spelling Board, which was organized in New York in 1906 "to promote, by systematic and continued effort, the gradual simplification and regulation of English spelling." Espoused by such men as Mark Twain, Henry Holt, Nicholas Murray Butler, and William James, the Board was financed by Andrew Carnegie; and it undertook one of the most ambitious efforts ever made for the reform of spelling.

It went into action in March 1906, with the publication of a list of words spelled in the simplified form. These simplifications were not radical. There were hardly enough words in the list to affect the appearance of any printed page—only three hundred words out of the hundreds of thousands in the language. Furthermore, not one of the proposed spellings was completely new. Most of them were already recognized by reputable dictionaries, at least as permissible spellings, and were already in fairly wide use. For example, *program* for *programme* and *catalog* for *catalogue*.

Simultaneously with the publication of this list, the Board began a promotional campaign intended to drive from the language the longer forms of the words and to establish the shorter ones. Despite some opposition, huge segments of the public responded enthusiastically to the campaign. In little more than a year the Modern Language Association, the National Education Association, and thousands of colleges and public school systems approved of the simplifications. So did the editors of the Webster, Century, Standard, Oxford, and other dictionaries. At the same time nearly 300 newspapers and magazines began using the simplifications; and so did more than 2000 business firms, employing them both in correspondence and in advertising. President Theodore Roosevelt ordered the use of the "new" spellings in all publications issued by the Government Printing Office.

Though attempts to reform English spelling had been made repeatedly since at least the year 1200, no attempt had ever gained so much momentum as this one.

The Board believed, therefore, that the public was ready for further simplifications, and published a Second List in January 1908. This one was more radical than the first. It had, not three hundred words, but more than five times that many; and instead of limiting itself to spellings that were already fairly well established, it included some that were new. For example, it clipped the final *e* from words like *native*; it threw out the *ig* of words like *foreign*; and it changed into a *t* the *ped* of words like *clipped*. "Thus clipt, nativ words lookt foren or defectiv."

Because of these more drastic changes, the Second List was not as popular as the First. Scores of magazine articles and newspaper editorials attacked it, and public enthusiasm "decreast" sharply.

Despite this lessening of enthusiasm, in January 1909 the Board published a Third List. Its simplifications—including *hed* for *head*, *livd* for *lived*, and *trimd* for *trimmed*—were even more extreme. They were so "trimd" that general approval of the movement not only "decreast"—it "ceast." It was overwhelmed by opposition which Professor Brander Matthews, one of the proponents of simplification, described as "rancorously and contemptuously hostile."

And thus ended what was perhaps the greatest campaign ever made to reform spelling. Today, about forty years after the supreme effort of the simplifiers, the accomplishments of the Board seem negligible. About nine tenths of the "long" forms which the Board tried to drive from the language with its First List still remain in acceptable usage. Clearly, then, even a policy of extreme moderation can produce only negligible results. Clearly, then, the present chances for reform are slim.

The fundamental reason, explain the opponents of reform, is simple: it is easier for people to spell and read in the "old" way than the "new." The "old" way harmonizes perfectly with all the complicated reflexes involved in reading and writing; the "new," on the other hand, upsets these reflexes and arouses their resistance.

Henry Holt, the publisher, discovered this fact when he sent to an elderly lady in Boston a letter which was carefully spelled to conform to a list of simplifications. This lady, who was a member of the elite on Beacon Hill and whose "dearest substitute for a daughter" Holt had recently married, was repelled by the letter. She cried out in agony to her son: "Florence has married a man who doesn't know how to spell!" A great many other people habitually consider the simplified versions of words, not as signs of the intelligent reformation of an inefficient system of spelling, but rather as signs of outright ignorance, ill-breeding and stupidity.

Another reason that attempts at reform are opposed is that the new spellings interfere with the connotations (or mental associations) which habits have built up around the words. *Buty,* to rhyme with *duty,* does not evoke the same associations as *beauty.*

It iz a buteus evning cam and fre

does not evoke the same responses as Wordsworth's

It is a beauteous evening calm and free.

Sometimes simplification not only removes the old associations, but also replaces them with new ones that are ridiculous or offensive. Sir William A. Craigie, who was knighted for his editorial work on dictionaries, implied that most knights would not like to be referred to as *nites*, much less as *nits*.

Because simplification thus disturbs associations and suggests illiteracy, it is usually avoided by publishers, teachers and other groups who exert the strongest influence upon spelling. Few publishers care to antagonize their readers with words spelled in a strange way, and few teachers care to jeopardize their jobs by spelling like illiterates.

Thus, despite the grotesque inefficiencies of the present system, the reformers are able to do very little about it. No matter how sleek and streamlined a new system might be and no matter how many rational advantages can be pointed out for it, the reflexes of the populace still resist. As a matter of fact, the more reasonable the system is—that is, the more it departs from the present standard of spelling—the greater is the resistance to it, for a greater number of reflexes rebel. Bad as it is, the present system may last indefinitely, just as traditional Chinese, another highly impracticable system, has lasted. The linguistic reflexes involved in reading and writing just don't tolerate the "od" and "nu-fangld."

part III

Wherein Are Capriciously Treated
Some Profound Problems, and Humor Has
Its Say

Robert Benchley

The Lost Language*

At the meeting of the International Philologists'
Association in Lucerne last April (1923–1925),
something in the nature of a bombshell was thrown
by Professor Eric Nunsen of the University of Ul-
holm. Professor Nunsen, in a paper entitled, "Aryan
Languages: The Funny Old Things," declared that
in between the Hamitic group of languages and the
Ural-Altaic group there should by rights come another and hitherto uncharted group, to be known as
the Semi-Huinty group. Professor Nunsen's paper
followed a number on the program called "Al Holtz
and His Six Musical Skaters."

According to this eminent philologist, too much
attention has been paid in the past to root words.
By "root words" we mean those words which look
like roots of some kind or other when you draw pictures of them. These words recur in similar form in
all the languages which comprise a certain group.
Thus, in the Aryan group, compare, for example,
the English *dish-towel*, Gothic *dersh-terl*, German
tish-döl, Latin *dec-tola*, French *dis-toil*, Armenian
dash-taller, Sanskrit *Dit-toll* and Dutch *dösh-tööller*.
In all of these words you will note the same absurdity.

In the same manner it is easy to trace the similarity between languages of the same group by noting, as in the Semitic group, that the fundamental
f in Arabic becomes *w* in Assyrian, and the capital

* "The Lost Language" from *Inside Benchley* by Robert Benchley. Copyright, 1942, by Harper & Brothers.

G in Phoenician becomes a small *g* in Abyssinian. This makes it hard for Assyrian traveling salesmen, as they have no place to leave their grips.

In his interesting work, "The Mutations of the Syllable *Bib* Between 2000 and 500 B.C.," Landoc Downs traces the use of the letter *h* down through Western Asia with the Caucasian migration into Central Europe, and there loses it. For perhaps two thousand years we have no record of the letter *h* being used by Nordics. This is perhaps not strange, as the Nordics at that time didn't use much of anything. And then suddenly, in about 1200 B.C., the letter *h* shows up again in Northern Ohio, this time under the alias of *m* and clean-shaven. There is no question, however, but that it is the old Bantu *h* in disguise, and we are thus able to tell that the two peoples (the Swiss and that other one) are really of the same basic stock. Any one could tell that; so don't be silly.

Now, says Professor Nunsen, it is quite probable that this change in root words, effected by the passage of the Aryan-speaking peoples north of the Danube, Dneiper and Don (the "D" in Danube is silent, making the word pronounced "Anube"), so irritated the Hamitic group (which included ancient Egyptian, Coptic, Berber and Otto H. Kahn) that they began dropping the final *g* just out of spite. This, in the course of several centuries, resulted in the formation of a quite distinct group, the one which Professor Nunsen calls the Semi-Huinty." It is not *entirely* Huinty, for there still remain traces of the old Hamitic. Just *semi*-Huinty. Even *semi* is quite a lot.

This, of course, takes no notice of the Ural-Altaic group. That is quite all right. No one ever does.

This group includes the Lappish, Samoyed, Magyar and Tartar, and, as Dr. Kneeland Renfrew says in his "Useless Languages: Their Origin and Excuse": "There is no sense in bothering with the Ural-Altaic group."

So Professor Nunsen has some authority for disregarding the question of grammatical gender, and it is on this point that he bases his discovery of the existence of the Semi-Huinty languages. These languages, he says, are monosyllabic and have no inflections, the tone used in uttering a word determining its meaning. In this it is similar to the Chinese tongue, which is one of the reasons why China is so far away from the European continent.

Thus the word *reezyl*, uttered in one tone, means "Here comes the postman," in another tone, "There is a button off this pair," and, in still a third tone, "you" (diminutive).

It will be seen from this how difficult it is for the philologist to do anything more than guess at just what the lost languages were really like. He is not sure that they are even lost. If they were *not* really lost, then the joke is on Professor Nunsen for having gone to all this trouble for nothing.

CLIFTON FADIMAN

Party of One*

A defense of the art of punning,
by an incorrigible practitioner

I have been hearing of late from certain readers who take a somewhat dimmer view of pun-making

* Reprinted from "Party of One" by Clifton Fadiman in *Holiday*, August, 1953, by permission of the author and of *Holiday* magazine.

than I do. I propose the following armistice terms: if my opponents will permit me to defend it briefly, I will promise henceforth never to exercise the art in these columns. Well, hardly ever.

There is something to be said against puns and I am not the man to say it. I admit that a pun derails one's train of thought. To some it is a sign that your words rather than your thoughts are being heeded. It upsets the dignity of speech, flouts the etiquette of serious communications, cuts the ground from under us. Our obligatory groan serves not only to convey a judgment but to cover discomfiture.

Furthermore, while to Christopher Morley a pun is language on vacation, to the non-punster it may seem more like language in agony. The contortionist repels even while he interests; so may the punster offend by the very ingenuity of his attack on language. That is, he offends because *he* commits the assault and battery before you do. *Meum* is not *tuum* but *tuum* may be mayhem.

The pun-hater abhors what the pun-lover rejoices in. The pun-lover doesn't mind interruption. Every time Noah Webster takes a prat-fall he is filled with glee. Indeed he *prefers* language under a strain. Let's take a test case. In *Animal Crackers* Groucho Marx recalled that when shooting elephants in Africa he found the tusks very difficult to remove—adding, however, that in Alabama the Tuscaloosa. To the contrapuntalist such a statement is quite irrelephant; to the pun-lover it is pleasing because it shows what language can produce under pressure. In this particular example language shows both the marks of strain and the strain of Marx. I will give you another. A few months ago on a television show called *This*

Is Show Business George S. Kaufman got himself mired in the word *euphemism*. After playing with it for a few seconds he turned to his fellow-psycho-panelist Sam Levenson, declared "Euphemism and I'm for youse'm," and closed the discussion. Now this, like Tuscaloosa, was pure purposeless play, art for art's sake, like doodling, whittling, singing in the bathroom and chewing bubble gum. It pleases the pun-lover precisely *because* of its denial of meaning. It has the charm of nihilism. . . .

Let's look at a few exhibits, drawing them from both the past and the present.

The simplest pun is based on the re-use of a word with a slight shift in meaning: S. J. Perelman's "Doctor, I've got Bright's disease and he's got mine." A pun involving not the slightest verbal distortion may have great richness. Take Sydney Smith's famous remark. Observing two housewives screaming at each other across a courtyard, he remarked that they would never agree because they were arguing from different premises.

Slightly more complicated than the identical-word pun is the Homonym. Here the words match in sound but not meaning. The homonym pun is the basic pun. Shakespeare used it almost exclusively; as children we cut our punning eyeteeth (known as *bon mot*-lars) on it. It may be quite plain, like Alexander Woollcott's title for a collection of his theater reviews: *Enchanted Aisles*—which might also have been called *Alec in Wonderland*. I submit a home-grown sample of the homonym, plain:

The Prideful Tern, about to be a mother,
Reflects that two good Terns deserve another.

Or, though plain, it may boast a fancy frill: "Days of Damon and Knights of Pythias" (O. Henry). It may be as fantastic as this classic by Christopher Morley. He and the late William Rose Benét were looking into the window of a wig shop showing two small wigs on their stands. "They're alike as toupees," said Mr. Morley.

The homonym may be broken up, like light passing through a spectrum. Groucho Marx, in the original stage version of *The Coconuts*, introduced the orchestra leader as follows: "This is Emanuel. I got him from Emanuel Training School. He's Emanuel like." It may be farfetched and yet perfectly homonymous, as in Ogden Nash's story of the hater of spring who appreciated the fact that his wife shot him with an autumnatic.

When the homonym is imperfect a certain wild touch of imagination is often present. Such puns depend on distortion. The distortion may be of varying degrees of complication. Change a single sound and you get Oliver Herford's "The more waist, the less speed." Change two letters and you get a name for New York's doctor-infested Park Avenue: Malady Lane. Change a syllable: "The audience strummed their catarrhs" (Woollcott). Introduce an additional syllable: "The things my wife buys at auction are keeping me baroque" (Peter De Vries in an amusing *New Yorker* story about a compulsive punner).

So far we have been considering only single puns, depending on one word. We begin to approach real structural complication when we get to double puns, whether homonymous or near-homonymous. Here's a good double pun of the kind that was fashionable in 19th Century America. At a dinner party a young lady was energetically flirting with her partner, whose name was Nathaniel. Her hostess-mother was listening with equally evident pleasure to the compliments of a Mr. Campbell. Noticing her daughter's over-apparent liveliness, the mother frowned in severe re-proof, upon which the daughter sent up a folded note on which she had written:

> Dear Ma, don't attempt my young feelings to trammel,
> Nor strain at a Nat while you swallow a Campbell.

(Of course for full effect Campbell must be pronounced in the English manner.)

Here is a well-constructed contemporary homonymous double pun, the handiwork of Sterling North: "A bustle is like a historical romance: both are fictitious tales based on stern reality." This is wittier than it is funny; I now offer one that is funnier than it is witty, from S. J. Perelman's *Horse Feathers*. The secretary, who has been holding a caller at bay in the anteroom for some time, warns Groucho, "Jennings is waxing wroth," to which Groucho replies, "Never mind. Tell Roth to wax Jennings for a while."

When the homonyms are off-beat and require a double-take from the listener, they acquire some of the uncanny charm of echoes. Here is a first-rate doublet of this sort by F. P. A.: "If you take care of your peonies, the dahlias will take care of themselves."

Triple puns are as rare as tartar steak. Kipling somewhere refers to Persian as a language so constructed as to make triple-punmaking a common pastime. Our own language, though flexible enough, is not quite so accommodating. Yet triple plays bob up once in a while, as flashy and memorable as comets. There is *Punch's* comment on the wit who complained that he was always hearing his own stories told back at him: "A plain case of the tale dogging the wag." In a recent *Trade Winds* column in the *Saturday Review of Literature* Bennett Cerf quotes an elaborate triple by the eminent advertising mogul Julian Brody. Mr. Brody explains why Pharaoh's daughter was like a shrewd, cold-blooded broker in a bear market. It's because she got a handsome prophet from the rushes on the banks. Triplets are ingenious but somehow not pleasurable. The contrivance behind them is too apparent, and their wit is efficient rather than meaningful.

The Meld Pun is especially characteristic of our times. Its most noted practitioner is undoubtedly Walter Winchell (*Reno-vate*, etc.). Mr. Winchell's coinages are often pointed, economical and witty. But his trick has been vulgarized by the kind of journalist who preens himself on such inventions as *cinemaddict* and *radiorator*. As Samuel Johnson remarked of Macpherson's poetry, any man can do this kind of thing who is willing to abandon himself to it. Such melds are as cheap as they are easy.

Nevertheless melds can be quite ingenious, as *alcoholiday* was in its time. Louis Untermeyer's term for composers who criticize and yet imitate Debussy —he calls them Debussybodies—is pretty. So is Christopher Fry's characterizing of a brilliant talker as "coruscating on thin ice."

To enjoy any art properly we learn to discriminate, inclining neither to wholesale rejection nor to uncritical acceptance. To drive the point home and demonstrate the delicate differences between a satisfactory pun and a brilliant one, I shall now ask you to consider four bits of wordplay. Each of the four is based on exactly the same word. The word is *dogma*. Even the nonexpert will see at once that the pun must turn on the simpler word *dog*. Give me a familiar phrase about a dog. Correct: *Every dog must have its day*. Our pun (it is Carolyn Wells') is at hand: *Every dogma must have its day*. Mildly witty but pretty simple. Let's see whether we can improve on it. We can do so easily with the help of Douglas Jerrold, who defined dogmatism as "puppyism come to its full growth." This is miles above Carolyn Wells. It makes a neater, more particularized statement about dogmas. In other words it has more meaning. Its construction, too, is far more interesting, involving a double pun, the second one turning on the literal and derived meanings of *puppyism*. The pun is first-rate. Can it be improved? I am not sure but I think I have one that's a shade finer. It's by Keith Preston:

A modernist married a fundamentalist wife,
But she led him a catechism and dogma life.

This also involves a double pun but a more unexpected one. Its statement is as meaningful as Jerrold's, both being pointed, sane comments on human life. It has the slight advantage over Jerrold's pun of being cast in rhyme. The form is a little tighter for that reason.

Have we exhausted the possibilities of *dogma?* Are you dogma-tired? Only one more to go, but this one is the real thing. Its author is Philip Guedalla, the English wit and historian. My recollection is that he was defending the Catholic Church (or perhaps some

other religious institution) from unfair and slander-
ous attack. He put it this way: "Any stigma will do
to beat a dogma." I consider this double pun, by
reason of the perfection of its form and the witty
truth of its content, one of the greatest ever made.
A man who can do that doesn't have to write a defense of puns. I do.

MORRIS BISHOP
The Impact of Beriberi on Walla Walla, Wash.*

All the folks who live in Walla Walla
    Love to execute the hula-hula,
Love to sing the ancient Eli Eli,
    Strangely harmonized with Boola-Boola.

Commonly their expletive is "Tút-tut!"
    And they like their garments with a froufrou,
Like to play a tomtom in a putt-putt,
    Call for chowchow, dining on the choo-choo.

Though they dose themselves with agar-agar,
    They are rather prone to beriberi.
Are they apprehensive? Not so very;
    As they put it, "Not so very very."

W. F. MIKSCH
Who Flang That Ball?*

My assignment was to interview Infield Ingersoll,
one-time shortstop for the Wescosville Wombats and

* © 1954 The New Yorker Magazine, Inc.
* Reprinted from *This Week* magazine by permission of the
author and the United Newspapers Magazine Corporation. Copyright 1951 by the United Newspapers Magazine Corporation.

now a radio sports announcer. Dizzy Dean, Red Barber and other sportscasters had taken back seats since the colorful Ingersoll had gone on the air. The man had practically invented a new language.

"I know just what you're gonna ask," Infield began. "You wanna know how come I use all them ingrammatical expressions like 'He swang at a high one.' You think I'm illitrut."

"No, indeed," I said. Frankly I had intended to ask him what effect he thought his extraordinary use of the King's English might have on future generations of radio listeners.

But a gleam in Infield's eyes when he said "illitrut" changed my mind. "What I'd really like to get," I said, "is the story of how you left baseball and became a sportscaster."

Infield looked pleased. "Well," he said, "it was the day us Wombats plew the Pink Sox . . ."

"Plew the Pink Sox?" I interrupted. "Don't you mean played?"

Infield's look changed to disappointment. "Slay, slew. Play, plew. What's the matter with that?"

"Slay is an irregular verb," I pointed out.

"So who's to say what's regular or irregular? English teachers! Can an English teacher bat three hundred?"

He paused belligerently, and then went on. "What I'm trying to do is easify the languish. I make all regular verbs irregular. Once they're all irregular, then it's just the same like they're all regular. That way I don't gotta stop and think."

He had something there. "Go on with your story," I said.

"Well, it was the top of the fifth, when this Sox batter wang out a high pop fly. I raught for it."

"Raught?"

"Past tense of verb to reach. Teach, taught. Reach,—"

"Sorry," I said. "Go ahead."

"Anyhow I raught for it, only the sun blound me."

"You mean blinded?"

"Look," Infield said patiently. "You wouldn't say a pitcher winded up, would you? So there I was, blound by the sun, and the ball just nuck the top of my glove—that's nick, nuck; same congregation as stick, stuck. But luckily I caught it just as it skam the top of my shoe."

"Skam? Could that be the past tense of to skim?"

"Yeah, yeah, same as swim, swam. You want this to be a English lesson or you wanna hear my story?"

"Your story please, Mr. Ingersoll."

"Okay. Well, just then the umpire cell, 'Safe!' Naturally I was surprose. Because I caught that fly, only the ump cell the runner safe."

"Cell is to call as fell is to fall, I suppose?" I inquired.

"Right. Now you're beginning to catch on." Infield regarded me happily as if there was now some hope for me. "So I yold at him, 'Robber! That decision smold!' "

"Yell, yold. Smell, smold," I mumbled. "Same idea as tell, told."

Infield rumbled on, "I never luck that umpire anyway."

"Hold it!" I cried. I finally had tripped this backhand grammarian. "A moment ago, you used nuck as the past for nick, justifying it by the verb to stick. Now you use luck as a verb. Am I to assume by this that luck is the past tense of lick?"

"Luck is past for like. To like is a regular irregular verb of which there are several such as strike, struck. Any further questions or should I go on?"

"Excuse me," I said. "You were saying you never luck that umpire."

"And neither did the crowd. Everyone thrould at my courage. I guess I better explain thrould," Infield said thoughtfully.

"Thrould comes from thrill just like would comes from will. Got that? Now to get back to my story: 'Get off the field, you bum, and no back talk!' The umpire whoze."

"Whoze?"

"He had asthma," Infield pointed out patiently.

I saw through it instantly. Wheeze, whoze. Freeze, froze.

"And with those words, that ump invote disaster. I swang at him and smeared him with a hard right that lood square on his jaw."

"Lood? Oh, I see—Stand, stood. Land, lood—it lood on his jaw."

"Sure. He just feld up and went down like a light. As he reclone on the field, he pept at me out of his good eye."

"Now wait. What's this pept?" I asked.

"After you sleep, you've did what?" Infield inquired.

"Why, slept—oh, he peeped at you, did he?"

"You bet he pept at me. And in that peep I saw it was curtains for me in the league henceforward. So I beat him to it and just up and quat."

"Sit, sat. Quit—well, that gets you out of baseball," I said. "Only you still haven't told me how you got to be on radio and television."

"I guess that'll have to wait," Infield said, "on account I gotta hurry now to do a broadcast."

As he shade my hand good-by, Infield grun and wank at me.

John Bailey

Definitions That May Be Right, or May Not*

LUMBAR REGION. Canada's northwoods.

PROFESSORSHIP. A ship full of professors.

IMPECCABLE. Any chicken with a stiff neck.

SUBSERVIENT. A servient who waits on people only in the cellar.

VALANCE. A female valet.

INTESTINE. To die without any airs.

REFINED. To pay the court another ten dollars.

CHILD-BEARING. Able to stand being around children.

FOLLY. To sneak after somebody.

MACADAM. The first Irishman.

RELYING. Telling the same story again.

CAPITULATION. To put your cap on.

PROWESS. A female prow.

HEADQUARTERS. Any quarters you find on your head.

NONCONDUCTOR. Anybody who doesn't work on a train.

FRESHET. Just finished eating.

PTARMIGAN. A pkind of pbird.

RHAPSODIST. One who wraps packages in a department store.

* Reprinted from "Definitions That May Be Right, Or May Not" by John Bailey in "Post Scripts," *The Saturday Evening Post*, October 2, 1954, by permission of the author.

NATURAL SELECTION. To take the largest piece.

UNTHINKABLE. A boat that ith airtight.

LATITUDINARIAN. Somebody who knows where he is up and down, but not sideways.

OFFLOOKER. An onlooker who is not paying attention.

SHELLEY. Shells everywhere.

INOCULATE. Too dumfounded to speak.

BEHELD. To have somebody hold you.

RICHARD B. GEHMAN

The Vague Specific*

The other day my wife woke me from a nap and said, "Say, what about all those things out in the front room?"

"What things?"

"Why, you know," she said, "those things. All that stuff."

She sounded as though she supposed I knew exactly what she meant. I didn't. For all I knew, "those things" could have been the furniture, books, rugs, magazines, lamps, or the remnant of a sandwich I'd been eating. I never did find out what she meant, because just then the telephone rang and she went to answer it.

I tell this rather pointless story because it actually has a point: It refers to an American conversational peculiarity—the habit, common mainly among

* Reprinted from "The Vague Specific" by Richard B. Gehman, *Collier's*, September 17, 1949, by permission of the author.

women, of referring vaguely to specific persons or things. I have named this the Vague Specific.

Women working together around the house are particularly addicted to this form of communication. Not long ago I copied down a conversation my wife and the maid had in the next room. It went this way:

"Here," my wife said, "you can take these."

"Where do you want them?"

"Oh, put them out there somewhere."

"With the others?"

"No," said my wife, decisively, "put them with those things behind the others."

The terrifying thing about this is that each knew exactly what the other meant. I can't explain this gift that women have, but I've analyzed it thoroughly and divided the Vague Specific into three general categories.

The first is the *Surrealist Vague Specific*. Once, from a distant room, my wife called to me:

"Say, come and do something about this box—it's rotten!"

Her words conjured up a picture reminiscent of a Salvador Dali painting: a headless torso, a melting watch, a rotten box.

"What do you mean?" I called.

"This box," she insisted, "is rotten!"

I went to investigate. The rotten box turned out to be an old window box, one that I'd been promising to fix. It was falling apart—but so far as my wife was concerned, it was rotten, so we threw it away.

This was similar to an experience suffered by a friend of mine, Arnold Uffelman, who appeared at my door one day looking haggard. "How about coming over and having a look at our washing machine?" he asked. "My wife says the thing on its side is acting funny." He sighed, and asked if I had anything to drink in the house.

After we'd fixed the washing machine—just a matter of readjusting the thing on its side—Uffelman and I fell to discussing this habit our wives have of being specifically vague. He thought of the second category: the *Vaguely Specific Individual*.

Uffelman's wife often turns to him and says something like, "What's the name of that fellow who drives the truck?"

Poor Uffelman knows of at least ten fellows who drive trucks, but he's never been able to think of the specific one his wife vaguely means.

I can sympathize with Uffelman, because all this is not unlike an announcement my wife sometimes makes to me when I get home from a tough cocktail hour at Pete's.

"The men came today," she says.

I never can tell which men she means, but I can never get up enough courage to ask. For a while, I had a system figured out to beat her at this game, but it backfired. The conversation went like this:

My wife: "The men came today."

Me: (Craftily) "What did you tell them?"

My wife: "I told them to go ahead."

The only satisfaction I got from this was the knowledge that, whatever the men had gone ahead and done, it was going to cost me money.

The third major category is the *Vaguely Specific Time*. I will list a few of these, with comments:

"Do you remember that time we were at the shore, and it rained?" (We've been to the shore 14 or 15 times; it's rained almost every time.)

"When was it that we had the Coes over?" (We've had the Coes over 12 times in the past two years.)

"What was the name of that couple we met the time we went to the Zeamers'?" (No comment here, except to point out the neat juxtaposition of the *Vaguely Specific Individual* and the *Vaguely Specific Time*. No mean feat.)

As I was saying, I can't explain all this. I thought I was on the trail of it the other day when I was reading a book on the psychology of American women, but just as I'd got to the second chapter my wife interrupted. "The woman's here for the money," she said. I gave the woman, whoever she was, her money, and then I went back to continue my reading—but somehow I couldn't find the book.

"Say," I asked my wife, "what happened to that book I had?"

For some reason, she didn't know what I was talking about.

PARKE CUMMINGS

What Was That Word?*

Several weeks ago I had my first indications that a change had come over Atherton, whom I had always regarded as an unusually garrulous person. We were strolling together when he pointed ahead of him. "Pretty woman," he remarked.

* Reprinted from "What Was That Word?" by Parke Cummings in *Collier's*, August 2, 1952, by permission of the author.

I nodded. "A honey of a babe," I said. "A dilly of a doll."

"A woman," said Atherton with a grim firmness in his voice. "A pretty woman."

"Sure," I agreed, puzzled. "That's what I said."

"Every intelligent man," declared Atherton, "owes it to himself to decrease his vocabulary."

"No question about that," I said. Then I did a double-take. "Did you say decrease? You meant increase, didn't you?"

"I meant decrease," he said. "When I call a woman a woman, I decrease or eliminate the word babe from my vocabulary. And that isn't all. During the last week I have also decreased my vocabulary by the words dame, doll, moll, Jane, broad, skirt and femme. Add those to babe, and that's eight words I've got rid of. With all those eliminated that would give me room to acquire something new—like avuncular."

"What's avuncular mean?" I asked.

"That's not the point," said Atherton. "The point is that I now have room to add avuncular to my vocubulary, if I ever get the urge to do so."

"But there's no limit to the number of words a person can learn," I objected. "You don't have to throw old ones out to make room for new ones—like apples in a barrel."

"That's all very well in theory," he retorted, "but in practice it just doesn't work out. Here's what happens when a man gets the habit of using babe, dame and all those other words for woman: he doesn't want to use the same one all the time—gives him a reputation for being monotonous—so he always has to stop and consider which one to use. Continually doing this is bound to entail a certain amount of wear and tear on his mind. Therefore he's just that much less apt to be sharp and ambitious enough to learn new—"

"I get your reasoning," I admitted, "but calling a woman a woman sounds coarse and crude."

Atherton nodded. "It was tough for me at first, but you get used to it if you persevere. Now I've got to the point where I can even say woman in the presence of—"

"Women?" I asked.

"That's right," he said. "Now take fried, crocked, squiffed, loaded, plastered, blotto, tiddled, soaked, boiled, stinko, oiled, polluted."

"Yes," I said.

"That's the next set of words I'm decreasing my vocabulary by," said Atherton. "Tossing them all out in favor of—"

"Intoxicated," I supplied.

"I favor drunk," said Atherton. "It's shorter and monosyllabic, even though it may sound a little harsher to the squeamish-minded."

"But there are degrees of difference," I objected. "Just being tiddled isn't the same as being blotto or—"

"When you get in the vocabulary-decreasing business," he interrupted, "you don't bother with technicalities. You throw out the whole kit and caboodle— I mean the whole bunch," he hastily corrected himself. "The Giants beat the Pirates yesterday."

"What's baseball got to do with this?" I demanded.

"They beat them," he repeated, "instead of wrecking, crushing, submerging, stopping, smearing, smacking, clobbering, murdering, sinking, creaming or chopping them."

"Or edging or shading them?" I suggested.

"Thanks," acknowledged Atherton. "That's two more I can throw out. Thompson made a home run. The initial bag, the keystone sack, the hot corner needn't enter into it."

"If you concentrate too much on decreasing your baseball vocabulary," I warned him, "you won't have time to concentrate on anything else."

"That's true," he conceded. "It's practically a limitless field."

"There's one thing I'm curious about," I said. "How does your wife feel about this new cult that you've taken up?"

"The old lady?" said Atherton. "The ball and chain? The better half? The ever-loving spouse? The helpmate? The old battle-ax? Well—"

"Do you realize what you're doing?" I shouted triumphantly.

"Don't rush me," said Atherton. "It may take years before I've finished this job completely. Besides," he added, "a fellow's got to draw the line somewhere."